FOCUS
Economic Systems

WRITING TEAM

Sarapage McCorkle

Bonnie Meszaros

Sandra J. Odorzynski

Mark C. Schug

Michael Watts, Chair

WITH AN INTRODUCTORY ESSAY BY

George Horwich

D1411388

NCEE

National Council on Economic Education

AUTHORS

Sarapage McCorkle
Director, Center for Entrepreneurship and Economic Education
University of Missouri-St. Louis

Bonnie T. Meszaros
Associate Director, Center for Economic Education and Entrepreneurship
University of Delaware

Sandra J. Odorzynski
Professor of Economics
Director, Center for Economic Education
St. Norbert College

Mark C. Schug
Professor of Education
Director, Center for Economic Education
University of Wisconsin, Milwaukee

Michael Watts
Professor of Economics
Director, Center for Economic Education
Purdue University

George Horwich
Professor Emeritus of Economics
Purdue University

FUNDING
The National Council on Economic Education gratefully
acknowledges the funding of this publication by the U.S.
Department of Education, Office of Educational Research and
Improvement, under PR Grant # R304A970001-98A. Any
opinions, findings, conclusions, or recommendations expressed in
this publication are those of the authors and do not necessarily
reflect the view of the U.S. Department of Education.

ISBN 1-56183-497-1

CONTENTS

FOREWORD

Focus: Economic Systems is the latest volume in a series of National Council on Economic Education (NCEE) publications dedicated to increasing the economic literacy of all students. The *Focus* publications, the centerpiece of NCEE's comprehensive **Economics**America program, build on over five decades of success in delivering effective economic education to America's students.

The *Focus* series is innovative, using economics to enhance learning in subjects such as history, geography, civics, and personal finance, as well as economics. Activities are interactive, reflecting the belief that students learn best through active, highly personalized experiences with economics. Applications of economic understanding to real-world situations and contexts dominate the lessons. In addition, the lessons are explicitly correlated to NCEE's *Voluntary National Content Standards in Economics* and *A Framework for Teaching Basic Economic Concepts*.

Focus: Economic Systems helps to reinforce the case for, as well as redefine the approach to teaching about different types of economic systems, in light of the breakup of the former Soviet Union and market reforms now underway in many nations that were, until recently, the most important examples of centrally planned economies. As demonstrated in the lessons contained in this volume, comparing the institutional arrangements that form the foundation of different nations' economic systems reveals that a wide spectrum still exists, ranging from largely individualistic and market-oriented approaches to a considerable degree of governmental intervention in the overall economy. In addition, there are still important examples of central planning and command economies that remain today which may be studied as part of a comparative economic systems course.

The development of this publication was undertaken as part of the International Education Exchange program funded by the United States Department of Education, Office of Educational Research and Improvement (OERI) under PR Grant #R304A970001-98A. NCEE extends its deep appreciation to the Department of Education for its support of this program. In particular, OERI program officer, Dr. Ram Singh, provided valuable advice and assistance. We are also grateful that the United States Congress had the foresight to realize the need for economic education in the emerging market economies and the vision to see how an international exchange program such as this could benefit U.S. students and teachers.

NCEE thanks the authors, Michael W. Watts, Professor of Economics and Director of the Center for Economic Education at Purdue University, who took the lead on this project; Sarapage McCorkle, Director of the Center for Entrepreneurship and Economic Education at the University of Missouri, St. Louis; Bonnie T. Meszaros, Associate Director of the Center for Economic Education and Entrepreneurship at the University of Delaware; Sandra J. Odorzynski, Director of the Center for Economic Education at St. Norbert College (Wisconsin); and Mark Schug, Director of the Center for Economic Education at the University of Wisconsin, Milwaukee. NCEE also thanks George Horwich, Professor Emeritus of Economics at Purdue University, for his enlightening introductory essay on economic systems.

Robert F. Duvall, Ph.D.
President and CEO
National Council on Economic Education

ACKNOWLEDGMENTS

The members of the writing team are grateful for the support from Patty Elder, Barbara DeVita, and other staff members at the National Council on Economic Education (NCEE) who commissioned this publication, and supported its development in many other ways.

Generous financial support to the NCEE from the U.S. Department of Education, Office of Educational Research and Improvement, for this publication and a wide range of other activities involving economic educators from the United States and over 20 transition economies, is also greatly appreciated.

George Horwich's essay was immensely helpful for us as we planned and wrote the lessons. We believe it will be an even more valuable resource for social studies teachers, and it was especially gratifying to see how well the essay was received by over 20 teacher/reviewers, listed here.

Our special thanks to Suzanne Becker for her careful, considerate, and comprehensive copy editing, and to Julie Huffer for her work in preparing camera-ready masters for the volume as well as handling uncounted administrative tasks on the project, great and small.

Finally, this publication was substantially improved by the following reviewers, including many classroom teachers who field-tested rough drafts of the new lessons on short notice and for little financial reward. Mary Suiter also offered valuable suggestions on several lessons.

Reviewers of the Complete Manuscript:

Thomas A. Pugel, Professor of Economics and International Business, Stern School of Business, New York University

Alexander Kovzik, Professor of Economics, Belarus State University

Dmitri Nizovtsev, Department of Economics, Purdue University

Reviewers and Classroom Field Testers of Selected Lessons:

Janice Boots, Bartlett High School, Anchorage, AK

Michael Brelick, Delcastle Technical High School, Wilmington, DE

Timothy Davish, Lakota East High School, Liberty Township, OH

Tracy Ann Devney, East Jessamine High School, Nicholasville, KY

Jim Flora, New Holstein High School, New Holstein, WI

Daniel Gatewood, Kilmer Alternative High School, Milwaukee, WI

Joy Joyce, Willowbrook High School, Villa Park, IL

Tim Matheus, Franklin High School, Franklin, WI

Robert Newgard, School District 170, Chicago Heights, IL

Tim O'Driscoll, Arrowhead High School, Hartland, WI

John Ostick, Malvern Prep, Malvern, PA

Sara Paul, Tartan High School, Oakdale, MN

Gerald Peden, Cape Henlopen High School, Lewes, DE

Steven Reff, University High School, Tucson, AZ

Todd Seelhorst, Smyrna High School, Smyrna, DE

Patricia Sheehan, Maplegrove High School, Minneapolis, MN

Amy Sutliff, Desert Mountain High School, Scottsdale, AZ

Leah Tesney, UMS-Wright Preparatory School, Mobile, AL

Ed Zippe, Alexis DuPont High School, Greenville, DE

PREFACE
TEACHING ECONOMIC SYSTEMS, WHY NOW, AND HOW?

With the breakup of the former Soviet Union and market reforms now underway in the nations that were, until recently, the most important examples of centrally planned economies, it is natural to ask why economists and educators should still teach courses or lessons on comparative economic systems. But a strong case can still be made for teaching about different types of economic systems, and the question then becomes how to teach that material most effectively.

Clearly traditional approaches to these topics, which typically featured detailed comparisons of institutional arrangements in Russia or other command economies to those of the United States or other market economies, are no longer appropriate without substantial updating and recognition of the much greater diversity that exists today across the transition economies. It has even become more difficult to justify extensive comparisons of Marxian economic, philosophical, and political thought with the writings of Adam Smith and other classical or neoclassical writers as the basis for lessons comparing different types of economic systems. Therefore, although core parts of the traditional approach to comparative systems are no longer relevant, it is perhaps less clear what the new focus of such materials and courses should be.

For those and related reasons, some universities have dropped their traditional comparative systems courses, and many more have retitled and restructured their courses to focus on the transition economies. In a 1995 *Journal of Economic Education* article, "The Future of the Comparative Systems Course in the Undergraduate Economics Curriculum," Clark G. Ross of Davidson College provides survey results and a general discussion of these issues. Ross found evidence that there is, indeed, less consensus about the appropriate content for new or modified courses on comparative economic systems or on the transition economies than there was for the traditional courses taught from 1950-1985. But he also makes a strong case that the comparative systems course and approach can provide many important benefits for students that are different from perspectives offered in other economics courses. That happens primarily because the comparative systems approach systematically links together concepts and material that are otherwise covered as relatively minor parts of many other courses, or not at all.

In broadest terms, what a comparative systems approach asks students (and instructors) to consider are such fundamental questions as: What is the economic basis for private or public ownership of land and other productive resources, and what are the consequences of different decisions about such ownership? What are the advantages and disadvantages of centralized and decentralized decision-making in the economy? What is the appropriate extent of, and what are the appropriate limits to, competition and legislated forms of cooperation in the economy? What are the basic functions of government in a market economy, given market failures such as public goods and externalities? Beyond those basic functions, how much more can government do in the economy if people demand such programs, and in particular how much income security and employment for workers in low-income families should the government try to provide? As the role of government has expanded even in market economies over the past century, how are special-interest problems created and dealt with in different kinds of economic and political systems? Finally, beyond all that, how much inequality of income is acceptable, given what is known about the mobility in labor markets where workers make most decisions about human capital investments and other career decisions?

A set of studies published by the National Bureau of Economic Research (NBER) found that even in the market economies of Western Europe, North America, and Japan, where institutions are not nearly as different as they are in comparing arrangements in these nations to the transition economies, different answers to these kinds of questions have led to very different results. Differences are found in employment and unemployment patterns; the degree of labor mobility and income inequality; the availability, structure, and effectiveness of vocational education and employee training programs; and perhaps even in rates of national output and income. (See the summary volume on these studies, *Working Under Different Rules*, Richard B. Freeman, ed., NBER and Russell Sage Foundation, 1994.)

What all of this means for this volume is that comparing institutional arrangements in different nations still reveals a wide spectrum, ranging from largely individualistic and market-oriented approaches to a considerable degree of governmental intervention in the overall economy, and especially in certain sectors of the economy. Therefore, a comparative systems approach will be useful in addressing the kinds of basic questions listed earlier, even after today's transition economies have completed their transition. But as long as the transitions continue – and all indications are that the transitions are far from complete in most of these nations – the potential for learning from the comparisons will be even greater, and the importance of teaching about them will remain even higher.

Because there are no standard courses or textbooks at the secondary level on economic systems, we commissioned an introductory essay on economic systems by Professor Emeritus George Horwich at Purdue University. This essay was enthusiastically received by all of the reviewers listed in the Acknowledgments,

and although the article was primarily intended as background information for teachers, a surprisingly large number of the teachers who reviewed it decided to use the essay as a student handout, too. The 12 lessons feature a wide range of activities, handouts, and discussion guides for classroom use. They were also well received by the teacher/reviewers, and cover many of the most important concepts and topics identified in the articles by Ross and Horwich. It is unlikely that any teacher will use all of the 12 lessons, and indeed some of the lessons are more likely to be used in economics or geography or world history classes.

Our hope is that many of the lessons will be used in classes where teachers want to teach about one of the most enduring questions of all human history: What kind of economic system delivers the goods, and the way of life, that people want most? Certainly that question largely shaped the economic and political history of the 20th century, and set the stage for monumental changes at the beginning of the 21st century.

INTRODUCTORY ESSAY
A COMPARATIVE ANALYSIS OF ECONOMIC SYSTEMS

George Horwich
Purdue University

CONTENTS

The twentieth century saw the rise and fall of an incredible variety of economic systems. They range from capitalist economies, in which most property and the means of production are privately owned, to socialist economies, in which most property is owned collectively and administered by the state. Capitalism is essentially a network of decentralized, price-directed, interdependent markets that spring up spontaneously. Government sets the rules and then intervenes only where market outcomes are judged to be inadequate or unacceptable. Socialism, in its pure form, is a centrally-planned command system in which government does most of the planning and commanding. In the last decade or two, the world's economies have swung sharply toward free markets, away from central planning and less extreme forms of state control. We shall survey these developments after defining what, in general, the economic problem is, what the essential elements of any economy are, and how well the basic goals of efficiency and equity are met by the alternative systems.

The Economic Problem and Its Solutions

An economy is an organized arrangement for producing goods and services to satisfy peoples' wants. The fundamental characteristic of any economy is the fact that the resources (land, labor, capital) available to produce those goods are limited or *scarce* whereas the wants are effectively unlimited. Hence choices have to be made. The economic problem is deciding what goods to produce, how to produce them, and for whom. The how of producing any good involves deciding – out of innumerable alternatives – which resources to use, in what combinations, and with what technology. In a word, the economic problem is deciding how to *allocate* scarce resources.

Because resources are limited and wants are not, producing any good or service means that some other goods people want can not be produced. Economists, therefore, define the *cost* of producing a good as the value of the next most valued good that was sacrificed in order to produce the good in question. This concept of cost – the value of forgone production – is referred to as opportunity cost. Notice that we have slipped the word value into the definition. What does it mean? In a market economy, the value of a good or service is the price established by buyers and sellers interacting in the market. Sellers decide how much to supply based on the cost of producing the product compared to the price they expect to receive for it. Demand is determined by the willingness of buyers to offer money for the good or service. Value is thus the outcome of a free "voting" process, where the votes are dollars of consumers' expenditures and sellers' receipts. In a centrally-planned command economy, where the primary allocation of resources is determined by planners, the value of goods and thus the costs of production are those of the collective society as perceived by the planners without reference to free-market prices. In a command economy that is politically democratic, these nonprice sources of information include elections and referendums regarding various government programs and expenditures.

Supply and Demand

The two extreme forms of economic organization can be characterized by supply and demand curves. A free market for a good or service is depicted in Figure 1(a), with price (p) on the vertical axis and quantity (q) on the horizontal. S is the market supply curve, and D the market demand curve. We can say that at each price, D tells us the quantity of the good buyers are willing to purchase and S indicates the amount producers are willing to sell. Alternatively, we can describe the schedules by saying that at each quantity, the corresponding point on D is the price that equals the additional value buyers receive from consuming that quantity, and the point on S is the price that must be paid to cover the additional costs of producing that quantity. Both ways of describing the curves are valid, but the second way makes explicit the relationship of supply to cost and demand to consumers' valuation. The curves typically have the upward and downward

slopes shown here because, as quantity increases, the cost of each additional unit tends to rise in the short run and the value of additional units consumed tends to fall.

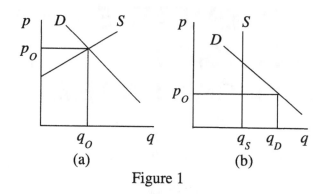

Figure 1

In a free market, price and quantity for each good or service will gravitate to the intersection of the supply and demand curves, the market "equilibrium," at (p_0, q_0). The price at that point is one at which the quantities supplied and demanded are exactly equal. At prices above (or below) the equilibrium, the quantity supplied would be greater (or less) than the quantity demanded and price would tend to fall (or rise) toward the equilibrium. At quantities above (or below) the equilibrium, the cost of producing any unit would be greater (or less) than the price consumers are willing to pay and quantity tends to fall (or rise) toward the equilibrium.

In the planned command economy, pictured in Figure 1(b), supply of any product is simply the quantity set by the planners, shown as the vertical line, S, unrelated to price. The demand curve, D, reflects consumer preferences, as in the market economy, but plays no direct role in allocating resources. Prices in centrally planned economies are not usually set at the market-clearing (supply-equals-demand) level. Instead, they are more often set at a lower price, p_0, as pictured, at which the quantity demanded by consumers, q_D, is greater than the quantity supplied, q_S. That creates an excess demand, equal to the distance $q_D - q_S$, also known as a *shortage*. Because quantity demanded exceeds quantity supplied, consumers acquire the good by resorting to ongoing search activity, queuing, doing favors for sellers, and other means, but not including the offer of a higher money price (which, in a command economy, would be an illegal bribe). Notice that if planners set prices above the equilibrium, there would be a surplus amount, $q_S - q_D$, *greater* than what consumers would be willing to buy. As a result, unsold goods would pile up on store shelves – an embarrassing situation for the managers of the enterprise. Generally, the goods that are overpriced in this sense and remain unsold are those of extremely poor quality, which consumers will not buy at any price. Unlike prices in free markets, prices set by planners in a command economy are fixed and do not adjust by market forces to the equilibrium level.

Information

In a free-market economy, prices transmit key information about the allocation of resources. Increased demand for a good causes its demand curve to shift to the right. This raises the price of the good, which, in turn, raises the demand for, the prices, and eventually the amount of resources used in its production. As resources are shifted away from producing products that have not experienced increased demand and prices, the production of the initial good will increase along the path of its supply curve.

Prices also change to reflect new information about the supply of a product. For example, a technological innovation will lower the costs of producing a good and thus increase its supply, shifting the entire supply curve to the right. At the old equilibrium price, the amount supplied is now greater, causing the price to fall and the quantity to rise along the given demand curve until reaching the intersection with the new supply curve.

The general character of the response to changes in the supply or demand for existing goods is fairly straightforward. For a new product, however, determining the price that consumers will pay and producers will accept is more complicated. Sometimes this information is garnered through market surveys. Often the discovery process is simply one of buying or selling new products on a trial and error basis.

Trial and error experimentation – consumers seeking their optimal mix of goods and services and producers seeking the least-cost methods of supplying them – is, in fact, a characteristic of most free-market activity. And in a free economy, one major source of information for consumers is the example of other buyers, whereas producers carefully watch the behavior of their competitors, both those that succeed and those that fail.

A vital link in the information process in market economies is the marketing of products, and specifically their advertising. Prices convey information about the terms on which products can be acquired only if consumers know that the products exist and what their features are. Advertising, even when not totally accurate in its claims, helps to indicate what the range of alternative products is. Advertising spreads information broadly and tends to increase competitive pressures on prices and product quality. Numerous studies of markets in which advertising is banned or severely limited indicate that the prices tend to contain a significant local-monopoly premium based on consumer ignorance. This premium, raising prices as much as 25 percent or more, is typically far greater than any price increase due to the cost of advertising (Benham, 1972, p. 344). Advertising is somewhat less important in the markets for industrial materials and capital goods where the buyers and sellers are fewer in number and producers study their supply sources as full-time professionals. Advertising and other marketing techniques play little or no role at all in centrally-planned economies, where firms are state monopolies and consumers have no direct role in determining what is produced or what its price will be. One of the clearest visible differences between a centrally-planned and a free-market economy is often the absence of billboards and other forms of advertising in the centrally-planned systems.

The price changes caused by supply and demand shifts provide relevant information directly observable by the affected parties. Moreover, in considering what to buy, consumers need to know *only* the prices of the goods they want and of close substitutes. Resource owners, producers, and potential producers of a product need only to know the costs of producing the product and its likely selling price. Even when a supply or demand change reverberates throughout the economy, the necessary adjustments in each impacted market can be made by the people directly affected by it, using information readily available to them.

Central planners, on the other hand, are responsible (in principle) for making all the adjustments throughout the economy in response to any and all changes in demand or supply conditions. To do this they must try to build a vast blueprint of all industries, indicating all the available resources, the multiple resource inputs required by every industry, each industry's possible outputs, the many alternative technologies for using resources, and the ranking of all consumer preferences. As a practical matter, no one can possibly secure and store all the information a completely informed central planner might want to have. Even if all the relevant facts had somehow been gathered and fed into a supercomputer, the data would quickly become obsolete as the inevitable daily changes occur in consumer tastes, available technology, and resource characteristics (such as the age and skills of the labor force, the vintage and capabilities of factories and machines, etc.). The central planners of the former Soviet Union, a country of several hundred million people, were able to specify the inputs and outputs of, at most, several thousand leading commodities. From this broad determination, regional planners established input-output relationships for their particular industries that would be consistent with the central plan. The industries, in turn, invited their individual enterprises to suggest their own input quotas that would mesh with the industry totals (Kohler, 1992).

In spite of the best efforts of the planning authorities to achieve consistency, inputs, except in the most strategic industries, were rarely adequate or appropriate to producing the specified outputs. As a result, much of the Soviet economy became a collection of informal markets in which enterprise managers sought inputs from each other while trying to meet their output quotas. Transactions were carried out with money, but at prices that did not, except in a few agricultural markets, reflect individual supply scarcities or buyers' demands. Instead, these prices were usually set below market-clearing levels to secure other – often macroeconomic – goals. The aim might be to control inflation or the amount of purchasing power to be received by selected groups of workers or households. Or, to facilitate planning procedures, prices might reflect average costs of production *excluding* rent and other implied returns to capital, because such payments were considered politically unacceptable. With prices fixed below market-clearing levels and unable to signal changes in the availability of resources, managers, like consumers, resorted to the extended search activity of a shortage economy as they looked for raw materials and other inputs. They relied heavily on word-of-mouth information and, in place of price adjustments, developed personal relationships that involved the exchange of goods for other goods (barter) or mutual favors (Litwack, 1991, p. 80).

Efficiency and Equity

Every economic system can be evaluated in terms of two fundamental attributes: efficiency and equity. Efficiency is measured by the value of the economy's total output per unit of resource input. The greater that ratio, the greater the efficiency. Equity refers to the "fairness" associated with the economy's allocation of resources. For example, how equal is the resulting distribution of incomes compared to how equal we think it should be? The answers to such questions, and hence the perceived equity in an economy, will be largely subjective in that they depend on people's ethical norms, political beliefs, and even religious views. The answers will also depend on a society's view of the nature of human behavior – for example, whether individuals are regarded as exercising free will with reasonable control over their circumstances or, instead, as being victimized by circumstances for which they cannot reasonably be held accountable.

Efficiency is less often seen as a subjective concept, but, as with equity, the notion of efficiency varies in different economic systems. The use of the word value in its definition immediately identifies efficiency with a particular point of view or ideology. For example, communist nations, such as the former Soviet Union and ancient Sparta, strongly preferred domestically produced goods to imports, which they felt made them unnecessarily and dangerously dependent on foreign suppliers. Soviet planners also considered heavy industrial output as far more valuable and critical to their well-being than consumer goods and services. Services were not even included in the official calculation of gross domestic product of the former Soviet Union. Marxian doctrine, which holds that labor is the source of all value, led the Soviets and other Eastern European economies to create extraordinarily high labor/capital ratios in their industrial plants, and to enforce a state of full employment in which no one was ever unemployed, even temporarily. The number of plants in the Soviet-type economies was also relatively few and their size consequently huge in order to simplify the task of central planning (Lipton and Sachs, 1992, pp. 30-32; Kroll, 1992, pp.161-162). The benefits of smaller and more numerous specialized units, even if known to the planners, were outweighed by the difficulties of planning for a greater number of factories.

With such differences in values, comparison of the output and hence of the efficiency of the Soviet economy with the Western economies had limited meaning. The capitalist economies tended to embrace foreign trade and achieved, through international specialization, high levels of output. But the Soviet state saw this as compromising the more important goal of economic independence. In the same vein, although large corporations in market economies all over the world have downsized their labor forces drastically in response to the electronic information revolution, Soviet-style economies would have been severely conflicted by such a development. Downsizing labor would have violated the Soviet commitments to high labor/capital ratios and to zero unemployment. Unlike the Soviets, capitalist economies are willing to tolerate temporary unemployment and restore full employment through the operation of their labor markets. The collapse of the Soviet Union in 1991 and its move toward capitalism can be interpreted as a massive shift of the Soviet peoples to the Western way of valuing output and assessing efficiency.

Incentives

Every economic system relies on an incentive structure – the ways to motivate consumers and producers alike to carry out their activities with diligence. In capitalist economies, prices motivate efficient behavior in several ways. Workers seek jobs that pay high wages and other benefits for their services. Consumers, informed by advertising, seek to pay the lowest product prices possible, thereby enhancing their *real* incomes. Firms try to get the highest prices they can for their products while minimizing costs, thus maximizing profits. Competition serves to hold prices down for both resources (inputs) and outputs. Lenders of investment funds – banks and other capital-market institutions – also oversee and monitor firm behavior to protect their investments and maximize their own profits. These are powerful forces – informed consumption, profit maximization, competition – and have, by common consensus, played a major role in the economic success of the capitalist economies.

Citizens in the centrally-planned command economies do not benefit so directly or systematically from their economic efforts. Consumers navigate as best they can in the shortage economy, but have no direct influence on prices, quantities, and the quality of products. Workers and managers are exhorted to be productive on patriotic grounds, but the rewards are less likely to be in wages and more frequently to be occasional bonuses, official honors, awards, and, for an elite few, special housing and buying privileges. The credo of most communist economies is the Marxian maxim, "From each according to his ability, to each according to his need." But the willingness of individuals to work selflessly while a higher authority gauged their "needs" and rewarded them in an uncertain, usually nonpecuniary manner, appears to have been a much less powerful motivator than capitalism's pursuit of individual self-interest.

In the centrally-planned economies, the state enterprises had the nearest earthly equivalent to eternal life. In economic terminology, they enjoyed "soft budget constraints," which means their expenditures were never limited to the revenues they raised though selling their products (Kornai, 1986). If their budgets were insufficient to cover their costs, because of uncontrollable external events or incompetent management, the enterprises were granted some combination of special subsidies and loans from the state banking monopoly or other government bureaus, permission to raise their prices, or exemptions from their tax liabilities. In the 74-year history of the Soviet Union, there is little or no evidence that a state enterprise was ever terminated or declared bankrupt (Lipton and Sachs, 1992, p. 33; Carson, 1997, p. 22). Nor were the central planners themselves subject to any systematic, external monitoring based on clear-cut economic criteria.

In market economies, the principle of satisfying consumer wants, also known as consumer sovereignty, is the ultimate object of economic activity. The principle is often violated by firms, unions, or government agencies that exercise some degree of monopoly power. But still the basic assumption is that consumers know how to spend their money to get what they want and that competitive private firms will know best how to produce and deliver those goods and services. In all of this, the paramount values are individual freedom and economic efficiency, as determined by market forces.

In centrally-planned, socialist economies, the emphasis is on equity and the achievement of a "just society" as reflected in the conditions of work and the distribution of income. In the former Soviet Union and in other, less repressive, collectivist societies, the primary goals have been zero unemployment, the end of workers' "alienation," and the equality of income. In the United States, the implicit credo – though not always enforced – is that people should bear the costs and consequences of their actions. There should be equal opportunity for all citizens, but not necessarily equal outcomes. And again, in theory if not always in practice, firms are as free to fail as to succeed. In the words of the famous Austrian economist, Joseph Schumpeter, bankruptcy – the weeding out of inefficient, unsuccessful firms – is capitalism's "creative destruction," its lifeblood and source of constant renewal.

Hybrid and Mixed Economies

There are, of course, no completely free-market or command economies. The freest of the capitalist systems have sizable government sectors. And even the former Soviet Union tolerated some private agricultural plots. After describing several forms of mixed systems, we will outline the economic basis for a significant government role even in a free-market economy.

Market Socialism

Market socialism is a combination of public ownership of all major industries and government control of investment, on the one hand, with price-directed market allocation of goods and resources, on the other hand. This post-Soviet blueprint for socialism recognizes the severe limitations of the centrally-planned command economy and tries to move beyond it. At the same time, it retains the vision of a just society by placing ownership of the means of production in government hands. This, it is believed, will remove the major source of income inequality by eliminating private profit in the most heavily concentrated industries. Meanwhile, managers at all of these firms, even though they are employees of the government, are instructed to hire resources, sell their products, and minimize costs using their own initiative under the guidance of freely determined market prices. In other words, managers are to behave like profit maximizers even though the profits they earn go to the government, not to them!

Though an improvement over command allocation, market socialism, in the eyes of its critics, suffers from the blunting of incentives due to public ownership. It is hard to imagine bureaucrats pursuing least-cost methods of production or the highest yielding investments with the fervor of someone in the competitive private sector. Only a private entrepreneur who has some chance of a large gain in a business venture will have an incentive to risk failure repeatedly and to try, try, and try again. Nor can banks or other private institutions, which perform the useful function of monitoring the performance of private firms they have financed, exercise any serious oversight over government agencies. Government is funded primarily out of general tax revenues, and even though it borrows from the public, including banks, it is accountable only to the voters. But the ballot box is a very infrequent, imprecise, and sometimes self-contradictory mechanism of social surveillance.

The world has never seen a true example of market socialism. Though the former republic of Yugoslavia referred to its economy in those terms, prices there were fixed by government decree and were not permitted to fluctuate in response to market forces. And profits were not maximized because workers participated in the management of enterprises and were more interested in paying themselves high wages than in minimizing costs. The People's Republic of China still characterizes its economy as market socialism, but profits of the now dominant nonstate enterprises go to investors, public or private, who have effective control of their company's resources and investment decisions.

Social Democracy

The social democratic economy leaves most property in private hands and hence is capitalist, but socializes many kinds of consumption. Several capitalist states, especially in Scandinavia and central Europe, fit this description. Also known as the "welfare state," government is responsible for providing so-called essential services and may, in some cases, nationalize a number of basic industries. Typically, government will provide health care, housing, schooling, retirement income, social services, day care, mass transit, and subsidies for the arts, and will nationalize railroads, airlines, coal, steel, and lifeline utilities, such as power, water, and telecommunications. Government itself is not necessarily the producer of these services, but instead, using public funds, it often purchases the outputs of private firms in these sectors and then distributes that output to consumers. But collective consumption cannot achieve the same degree of flexibility and precision in satisfying individual preferences that individual private buyers can, operating in a free market. For one thing, the collective buyer cannot possibly know or make the fine distinctions in product variety and quality that individuals would make for themselves. Nor can a large, visible public buyer hope to simulate the private individual's trial-and-error learning process. As a result, there will be a bureaucratic tendency to stay with given suppliers longer than justified and to resist innovation and competitive change.

State Capitalism or Mercantilism

State capitalism, sometimes called mercantilism, is a catch-all category that combines private ownership of the capital stock with extensive government involvement designed to serve not the consuming public as a whole, but rather the goals of politically influential interest groups. These include established ("crony") capitalists, organized labor and professional associations, farmers' lobbies, environmentalists, energy conservationists, and self-appointed consumer "advocates." Protection against competition (foreign and domestic) and limitations on immigration are common objectives of these groups.

Latin American governments have been notorious in the past for serving either the special interests of leading labor unions (for example, the mid-century Peronist regimes of Argentina) or capitalists (throughout the hemisphere). India has been highly protectionist in the past, and Japan continues to protect established firms in many sectors from both foreign and domestic competition. Labor unions and political parties in Western Europe have secured extensive regulation of labor markets, coupled with generous public support for day care and family leave for parents with young children. Though many consider these programs worthwhile, they result in higher levels of unemployment and lower levels of productivity.

Today, most economies have some elements of all the hybrid systems. It is a matter of judgment to determine which label fits a particular nation best. None of these categories, however, including central planning, provides a clear rationale for choosing between private and public provision of goods and services in an economic system. We turn now to that question, the role of government in economic activity.

Government, Public Goods, and Public Choice

Government's first responsibility is to establish a legal framework for society. In a free society, government provides a rule of law, which defines and enforces property rights and the law of contracts. Property rights pertain not only to physical capital and the right to use, develop, and transfer it, but also to the rights of individuals as economic agents. These latter rights include the freedom to earn income, to invest in one's own skills, to move freely in and out of different jobs, and to spend, save, and raise financial capital for investment.

Public Goods

Government's remaining responsibility is to produce, or encourage others to produce, goods that people want but the market fails to supply. Such goods are "public goods" and have the characteristic that they can only be consumed jointly; that is, once produced, they can be consumed freely by all whether they have paid

for them or not. Moreover, one person's consumption of the good does not deprive others of their consumption of the good. Examples of public goods are clean air or a wall protecting a country's borders against foreign invaders. As a result of public goods' joint consumability, private individuals are reluctant to pay for them. There is a strong incentive to wait for others to buy them first and then to be a "free rider." When everyone faces the same incentives and tries to free ride, demand for these products is present in individuals but fails to materialize in the marketplace. Without market demand, private producers will not supply the good.[1]

The way out of this impasse, after reaching a public consensus, is for government to be the demander, paying for public goods with tax revenues. Although private suppliers can produce most public goods, the government, having entered the market as the demander, may also become the producer. In the United States, this happened in the case of first-class mail delivery and the supply of military *services*. It did not happen with regard to war *materiel*, which the government buys from the private sector.

Given the nineteenth century goal of populating the American continent, universal mail service at a price well below the cost of private delivery was widely believed to be in the national interest and thus a public good. Universal service could have been accomplished by offering subsidies to private mail suppliers. But instead, the government created a postal monopoly in 1837 and delivered the mail itself. Economists have not generally accorded the government postal service high marks for efficiency. On the other hand, one would hesitate to buy military services from a mercenary who might be bid away by the enemy in the midst of battle! Hence, even if military services are seen as inefficient in a narrow economic sense, their importance appears to justify public ownership and control of the armed forces.

Macroeconomic stabilization, which is the control of inflation and the smoothing of the business cycle, is another public good, jointly consumed by everyone in a nation. But private means of accomplishing it are, at best, problematic. Government control of the monetary base and the tax system, the major tools of monetary and fiscal policy, seems to make government the least-cost producer of such services. As with all government-supplied goods and services, however, economists continue to debate how well government has actually performed its stabilization role.

Assuming majority approval in democratic societies, equity objectives such as reducing the inequality of income through tax policy can also be public goods because the electorate experiences joint satisfaction in them. And, as in macroeconomic stabilization, only the government is likely to control the resources to carry out these programs on the desired scale. But we must add the proviso, applicable to any public good, that despite the majority sentiment, the minority that oppose it must be judged not to be unduly harmed by it.

Protection of the environment is almost always a public good and requires active government involvement. From an economic perspective, the optimal strategy is to reduce pollution only to the point where the added social benefits continue to exceed the added costs, and no further. Where feasible, economists prefer to avoid across-the-board environmental regulations that apply equally to all persons and firms because it is much less costly for some polluters to abate than it is for others. When low-cost firms do a larger share of the pollution reduction, the total cost of environmental cleanup will be minimized. Society benefits from this approach because fewer plants are shut down and fewer jobs are lost in achieving any given amount of environmental protection. The way to reach this result is to give polluters a choice between paying a fixed per-unit tax on their pollution and reducing the amount they pollute. Then those for whom cutting back is more costly will do so to a lesser degree and instead pay the tax. An alternative scheme is for government to sell "licenses" to pollute, which will be purchased

by those for whom not polluting costs more than the licenses.

An interesting question arose after the collapse of the Soviet Union in 1991 – namely, why that country and its communist satellites in Eastern Europe were arguably the world's worst industrial polluters. There are three reasons – each revealing a basic economic phenomenon or principle:

(1) Their per capita incomes were low – on the order of $3,000 to $8,000 per year at a time when U.S. per-capita income was in the low $20,000's. It has been observed that countries do not spend a significant amount of money on pollution reduction until their annual per-capita income reaches $4,000 to $5,000.

(2) Based on decisions made by central planners in these countries, output was made up disproportionately of heavy industrial goods – a much greater source of pollution than the output of the more service-oriented capitalist economies.

(3) Because clean air and water are usually public goods that cannot be purchased by consumers in the marketplace, the demand for them in any society can only be expressed in open democratic forums, such as free elections and a free media. These were totally absent in the Soviet Union.

Government "Failure"

Although government is needed to facilitate the production and consumption of public goods, there are a number of inherent limitations in government activity, which may defeat that goal. Government agencies in market economies suffer from many of the same incentives and protections that characterize socialist enterprises and central-planning agencies: They do not have to pass a market test to survive and they are extremely difficult to oversee and monitor. There are no prices or other systematic information to value their output or assess their impact on the economy.

They have no competitors to force them or show them how to minimize costs, and their budget constraints are certainly soft. Very few U.S. government agencies have ever been truly terminated. They are more likely to be merged with other agencies without surrendering their functions.

Democratically-elected governments generally score poorly on social efficiency criteria. They tend to be most responsive to groups that lobby government most intensely, and to enact policies that offer huge benefits to a concentrated few while spreading the costs in small amounts among the many. Voters in democratic elections cannot usually vote the intensity of their preferences. No voting scheme, in fact, can approach the continuous, flexible, precise expression of preferences available to consumers in a price-directed free market. Instead, elections usually bundle thousands of choices covering a multitude of decision areas into a single, infrequent, up-or-down vote for a candidate or a party.

Three Major Economies and the Rest of the World

We turn now to an account of three of the world's major economies: the United States, a market system that is the world's largest and most productive economy, and two former centrally-planned command economies now moving to free markets – the People's Republic of China, in the midst of a gradual transition, and Russia, attempting a rapid transition. We conclude with a summary of several other transition economies in the world and Japan.

The United States[2]

In 1776 the United States was a nation of 2.5 million people in a land mass of 0.8 million square miles and with a per-capita gross domestic product (GDP) (in 1998 prices) of $1,600. More than 90 percent of the population were engaged in farming. By 1998, 222 years later, 270 million people were living in the U.S. in an area of 3.6 million square miles with a per-capita GDP of $29,000. Only 2.3 percent of the people were farmers. Because per-capita GDP

(corrected for inflation) had grown more than 15-fold and the population had increased 108-fold, the real GDP itself in 1998 was 15 x 108 or roughly 1,600 times greater than it had been in 1776. During this period the growth of real GDP averaged 3.4 percent per year, and the growth of GDP per capita, 1.24 percent per year. These are not explosive rates, but they accumulated significantly over time, particularly considering the enormous quality improvements in output (such as totally new products and technologies) that are not fully captured by the statistics. What is unique about the U.S. experience in this period are the sheer magnitudes involved. While the U.S. population soared (an increase of 108 times), that of Western Europe increased by a factor of only four. The U.S. population increased both because of high birth rates and because of an unprecedented flow of immigrants, first from Europe and Africa (slaves), and eventually from all over the world.

There is no evidence that the U.S. distribution of income has changed drastically from colonial times – in other words, the increase in income was a "rising tide that raised all boats." The per-capita incomes of all household quintiles (each with 20 percent of the population), ranked from richest to poorest, are, roughly, 15 times greater than they were in 1776. There were, of course, periods in which the degree of inequality fluctuated, with some quintiles gaining more income than others. In the nineteenth century inequality seems to have increased; then, from 1929 to the 1970s, it decreased. In the 1980s and 1990s, inequality rose because of the increased return to higher education, caused in large part by the information revolution. Where college graduates once earned 20 percent more over their lifetimes than high school graduates, the difference is now 75 percent and still rising (Katz, et al., 1995, chap.1). That seems to be a consequence of the introduction of computer technology throughout the economy, placing a greater premium on literacy. Historically, however, significant technological advances have tended to increase income inequality only for a limited time. Eventually the equipment becomes more user friendly, the less educated become more educated, and nearly everyone adjusts.

Today, at the height of the computer revolution, the average income of the highest quintile of households in the United States is 14 times greater than the average income of the lowest quintile, unadjusted for taxes or benefits provided by government spending programs. When incomes are expressed net of taxes and inclusive of benefits, both cash and in-kind, the ratio of high to low incomes falls from 14 to 4.

The single most important determinant of U.S. economic growth is technological change, at least in most decades of the twentieth century. On average, the annual 3.4 percent GDP growth rate is due in equal parts to: (1) new inventions and production methods, (2) increases in the existing varieties of physical capital and natural resources, and in the quantity and quality of the labor force; and somewhat less to (3) the reallocation of resources from less to more productive uses, which includes the ongoing movement of resources from rural to urban areas and the shift from smaller to larger firms and production methods (Denison, 1974, pp. 130-133; Mankiw, 2000, p. 129). Finally, it should be noted that the U.S. economy has not become less competitive over its history. The opposite seems to be true, both in manufacturing industries and the burgeoning service sectors (Gregory and Stuart, 1995, pp. 159-162).

China[3]

The People's Republic of China (PRC) was established in 1949 after communist forces led by Mao Zedong triumphed over the Nationalist army led by Chiang Kai-shek. All land and property, except for limited personal items, were nationalized by the end of the 1950s, but central planning and allocation were divided between regional authorities and the national government in Beijing. Unlike the Soviet Union, China was largely an agrarian country with at least three-quarters of its then half-billion population living on the land. The collectivization process in agriculture was also more decentralized.

Instead of creating massive collective farms, as in the Soviet Union, China combined small family plots into communes that controlled the agriculture of each township or village. The work unit – often the commune itself – became the controlling organization in the lives of the people, determining their job assignments and schooling, allocating housing, granting permission to marry and have children, administering a justice system, etc. Prices were strictly controlled and most economic activity was subject to direct command allocations.

Two cataclysmic government policies caused untold hardship. The first was the Great Leap Forward in 1958-62, which enforced agricultural and industrial self-sufficiency at every level, from communes and villages to the provinces. All trade was discouraged and the benefits from specialization and exchange were treated as pernicious capitalist myths. Communes were to grow their own food and villages were to produce as many of their own manufactured goods as possible. Land most suitable for growing certain crops was used for growing all crops, ruining the soils for years to come. "Backyard" foundries were built to convert iron into steel. The result was economic turmoil and history's greatest famine. According to the government's own statistics, 27 million people starved to death during this period.

The other catastrophic policy was the Cultural Revolution of 1966 to 1976, in which roving bands of young Red Guards attacked the elite citizenry – the educated, the highly skilled, the most accomplished members of the professions. Hundreds of thousands were arrested and beaten, often killed, in a great leveling purge. All universities were closed, with students and faculties sent to rural backwater communities to bring them closer to the "ordinary" people and to experience grassroots "socialist" life. Though casualties were much lower than in the Great Leap, the Cultural Revolution was demoralizing and, to say the least, socially and economically disrupting.

Mao finally died in 1976 and was succeeded by Deng Xiaoping as the paramount leader. Deng knew that the Chinese people were increasingly aware of the stunning economic progress taking place in the West and elsewhere in Asia. Particularly dramatic was the growth of free-market economies in neighboring Hong Kong – then a British colony but populated by many who had escaped from mainland China – and Taiwan, the island province to which the defeated Nationalist Chinese had fled in 1949. Deng had opposed the collectivization of agriculture in the 1950s, for which he had served the first of several prison terms. In 1978 he prepared to give the people a measure of the economic freedom they yearned for and might otherwise seize.

The first and most significant liberalization in the PRC was the effective breakup of the communes. Individual families were permitted to lease plots of land in the commune for limited periods of time. After meeting state quotas at set prices, they could grow any crop and sell it anywhere for whatever price it would bring. Over time, lease periods were increased and leases were made renewable and tradable. The effect on Chinese agriculture was dramatic. Farm output and income rose 60 percent in just six years. Because 30 percent of China's population, then a billion people, were engaged in farming, Deng had created the largest occupational constituency on earth – 300 million people – for his market-based reforms.

Almost simultaneously, 14 cities and five Special Enterprise Zones along the Pacific coast were declared open to foreign goods and capital. Foreign firms participated mainly in joint ventures with Chinese partners, but some also entered China as fully funded companies. Foreign investors were permitted to hire and fire labor as they saw fit and were taxed at minimum rates. Gradually, over the next two decades, the open areas were enlarged to include most of China, and managerial freedom was extended to all new enterprises. Most prices were freed and almost all command allocations ended.

Meanwhile, the huge productivity increases resulting from the agricultural reforms and the opening of the cities created a surplus labor force of 100 million workers. They soon found jobs in the many new joint ventures and so-called township and village enterprises (TVEs). The latter were new manufacturing plants built spontaneously in the countryside, funded by the savings of farmers and other citizens, by revenues of local and provincial governments, and by foreigners. Today the TVEs account for more than half of China's industrial output. Only 29 percent of output comes from state-owned enterprises (SOEs), which produced 78 percent of industrial output in 1978. Relics of the centrally-planned command economy, the SOEs are almost all heavily supported by government subsidies, and are failing even though their managers can be dismissed if they fail to earn a profit or at least reduce losses. The Chinese government would dearly love to liquidate the SOEs, but cannot because several hundred million workers and their families depend on them not only for jobs, but for housing, health care, and numerous other services not yet available outside the workplace. The long-term goal is gradually to shrink the SOEs to a tolerably small percentage of the GDP as the nonstate portion of the economy continues to grow.

How does China today meet the criteria for an effective free-market economy? China has never declared that the means of production – factories and other capital goods – are not publicly owned. Instead, it has granted investors absolute rights to the *income* generated by their investments, including the right to transfer or sell those rights. The government has acknowledged the legitimacy of private property, but has placed so many limitations on its use that most investors prefer to invest in loosely defined collectives, such as the TVEs.

The Chinese government can not indefinitely retain the myth of public ownership, however. Virtually all enterprises in China, including many SOEs, would like to be able to issue shares of stock, which is awkward under the present system. China has nevertheless been able to attract significant amounts of direct foreign investment, much of it from the 55 million Chinese living overseas. They and other private investors, many channeling their funds through Hong Kong banks, have acted as partial substitutes for the independent banking system and capital market that China still lacks and must develop. The banking system is, in fact, in serious danger of becoming insolvent as its loans to the SOEs increase. The SOEs, in turn, continue to depend heavily on subsidies from the central government, which can be maintained only if the government can significantly raise its tax revenues (Lardy, 1997).

On the inflation front, China's central bank has done a reasonably good job in recent years of reining in the price level. The social safety net has been slow to develop, but significant progress has been made in transferring ownership of apartments to their occupants.

Despite the ad hoc nature of its market reforms, and the problems it still faces, China's GDP has grown at an average annual rate of 7 percent since 1978. China's per-capita GDP was $614 in 1950 and rose to $1,352 by 1978. Today it is over $4,000, making China the world's second largest economy after the United States.

Russia

When the Soviet Union collapsed in 1991 the republic of Russia, with 150 million citizens representing about half of the former Soviet Union (FSU), embarked on an avowed course of free-market capitalism. Unlike China's gradual pragmatic approach, Russia adopted a formal, cold-turkey set of reforms that it hoped would create an immediately functioning free-market economy. Per-capita GDP in Russia in 1991 was more than five times greater than it had been in China in 1978 at the start of the Chinese reforms. In Russia and in the former Soviet republics, however, the institutions necessary for capitalism were far less developed and centralized planning was far more advanced. Nevertheless, there has been a great deal of progress in Russia, although the process has been far from smooth or steady.

Created in 1917 by the Bolshevik revolution, the Soviet Union has a history no less turbulent than that of the PRC. Civil war raged until 1920, accompanied by forced collectivization of agriculture and nationalization of enterprises. Money was considered a capitalist tool, and so it was banned and replaced by barter. Peasants were required to deliver crops to the government without compensation, and labor was conscripted and effectively militarized. Agriculture collapsed, industrial production fell 80 percent, and 12 million died in the ensuing famine. Thus occurred one of history's most brutal lessons on the importance of money as a medium of exchange and on the role of positive incentives in the allocation of resources. In 1921 a "New Economic Policy" was established, allowing a partial restoration of free markets, which revived the economy. But the NEP ended in 1928 with the ascendance of Joseph Stalin to absolute power. Fixed prices and central planning replaced virtually all free-market activity. Not until 1939 did the Soviet Union regain its 1917 level of GDP. World War II, in which more than 20 million Soviets lost their lives and at least a third of the capital stock was destroyed, was the country's greatest cataclysm.

Following the war the Soviet Union rebuilt its economy within the centrally-planned/command framework. By 1989, on the eve of the breakup, annual per-capita GDP had reached $7,078 or roughly a third of that of the United States. But as noted earlier, this comparison is not entirely meaningful. Output in the FSU was determined primarily by central planners, who did not follow consumers' preferences. A much greater fraction of Soviet GDP was devoted to defense expenditures – roughly 20 percent, compared to the U.S.'s 5 percent, leaving a smaller fraction for consumption (Aron, 1998, p. 8). Soviet goods were also of generally lower quality and, in the shortage economy, required endless search activity to find. A generous guess is that the Soviet standard of living, measured by U.S. criteria, was no more than a fourth of the U.S. level.

The collapse of the FSU was essentially nonviolent, and spurred by circumstances similar to those that initiated market-based reforms in the PRC. The growth of information technology made it impossible in either country to suppress knowledge of the free economies and the laggard state of the communist economies. For the FSU, most galling was the contrast between depressed, communist East Berlin and prosperous, capitalist West Berlin, which the wall could no longer hide. The aggressive American military buildup in the 1980s, which the Soviets felt they could not afford to match, was also a probable factor in the Soviet collapse.

Russia moved swiftly in the early 1990s to free all prices, privatize the capital stock, end its reciprocal state-trading relations with Eastern Europe, and open its economy to goods and investment from anywhere in the world. Prices soared, although the real cost of goods rose less because the move to market-clearing prices and quantities ended the shortage economy, its costly search activity, and its bare shelves. Consumer goods and services emerged spontaneously in a burst of entrepreneurial energy.

More complex was the process of privatizing the existing means of production. The plan was to issue equity shares to the public, which could be converted into ownership claims to selected SOE's or sold on the open market. From one-third to one-half of the shares of any company were to go to the employees – workers and managers combined. In fact, this group, preponderantly the former state managers, emerged with two-thirds of the shares of most enterprises (Aron, 1998, p. 5). From an efficiency, if not an equity, point of view, this outcome need not have been devastating. Once an asset is privately owned by someone, its optimal and de facto use tends to be independent of the particular owner.

Nevertheless, several factors continue to undermine the efficient allocation of resources: (1) political instability, reinforced by the weak financial status of the government, has weakened support for market reforms; (2) the failure to develop an independent banking system and capital market, or to attract substantial amounts of foreign investment, have left Russia without adequate enterprise-oversight institutions; (3) official corruption and mafia activity, both a carryover from the Soviet era, are widespread; (4) the absence of a social safety net has blocked efforts to liquidate and restructure the former SOEs, now in private hands but still receiving state subsidies and suffering from bloated labor forces and low productivity. All of these circumstances have slowed the transformation of the Russian economy.

Russia and China share many of the same problems. But unlike China, Russia does not have a huge population of expatriates and their descendants in other countries, willing and able to fuel a foreign investment boom in the mother country. And unlike China, Russia has not yet devised a way to break up its collective and state farms and privatize its agriculture. Finally, China remains an essentially stable political dictatorship, experiencing the first stirrings of electoral democracy only at the local level. Russia, with almost no history of political freedom, moved swiftly to free and open national elections in the early 1990s and has suffered, simultaneously, social, political, and economic unrest, slowing the transition to free markets (Aron, 1998, pp. 3-4).

In spite of all this, at a present per-capita GDP of $4,200, Russia *on average* is not obviously worse off economically than it was in the last several years of the FSU. As noted, the higher Soviet per-capita GDP was not based on consumers' choices, product quality was inferior, and a huge percentage of output was war materiel, which gave no direct benefit to consumers (Feldstein, 1997). And today the true Russian GDP is doubtless greater than the official figure, because there is a large unreported underground economy that pays no taxes, and is probably larger than the comparable illegal activity under the FSU. Whatever its level, the Russian GDP ended its decline and increased slightly in 1999. Nonpayment of taxes is, however, a serious problem for Russia's government, which narrowly averted bankruptcy in 1998.

The Rest of the World

Several of the former Soviet satellite economies are doing well. The per-capita GDPs of Poland, Hungary, the Slovak Republic, and the Czech Republic are well above Russia's at: $6,400, $7,000, $7,900, and $11,400, respectively. Poland and Hungary were never as centrally controlled as Russia, and Poland never nationalized its land, which remained privately owned. All of these countries have moved resolutely to establish private ownership, open their markets, and dismantle their socialist industries. East Germany, once again united with West Germany, is being economically integrated, but remains well behind its Western partner. The other Soviet-bloc countries, Romania and Bulgaria, are at about Russia's level and also moving slowly. The remaining former Soviet republics, such as Ukraine, are severely depressed.

Outside of China, other Southeast Asian economies were never centrally controlled and, in varying degrees they have abandoned mercantilism for a path to free markets. The Asian tigers – Singapore, Hong Kong (once again, part of China), South Korea, and Taiwan – have experienced phenomenal growth. The first two are among the highest income countries in the world, and the latter two are at the upper middle-income level. Malaysia and Thailand have also achieved solid middle-income status. Indonesia and the Philippines are low income but on a clear growth path, as is India, the world's second most populous country. The recent Asian economic crisis seems not to spring from any fatal flaws, but is rather a signal that the markets in these countries need further liberalization and an end to the crony capitalism and protectionism that their governments still practice.

The Japanese economy, which is the world's third largest, had a modest per-capita income of $1,873 in 1950. It soared to $11,017 by 1973 – driven by an unprecedented annual growth rate of 8 percent. It grew at 3.2 percent for the next 24 years, reaching $23,400 in 1997. But it has been essentially stagnant since the early 1990s, when its real estate and stock markets collapsed. Japan today is suffering both from an unduly stringent monetary policy and structural problems that can only be described as mercantilist. Its major manufacturing industries are cartels; its distribution and marketing network is tightly controlled and only occasionally open to new entrants. Although its exports are highly competitive in world markets, Japan has a degree of domestic communalism and egalitarianism that is unusual for an advanced economy. Japan, in fact, has espoused policies not unlike those of the centrally-planned economies: low to zero unemployment, limited to zero bankruptcy, and overall industrial policy or coordination. But Japan has an even longer history of capitalism and reliance on price-directed markets. In fact, the social and industrial policies have been circumvented or gradually relaxed. Firms not favored by the official policy have managed to secure funding from a porous banking system, lifetime employment is declining, and bankruptcy is growing. The phenomenal postwar growth seems to be a result of the low level at which Japan started, its highly skilled and motivated labor force, and an extraordinarily high rate of return on investment that, until recently, left a lot of room for market-constraining social policies.

Most of Latin America is undergoing steady economic liberalization. Western Europe, at the upper reaches of world income, is undergoing political and economic unification and will benefit from the common currency it is adopting. Africa, the last frontier of development, is beginning to stir.

Notes

1. An equivalent way to describe the phenomenon of public goods is in terms of externalities. The latter are costs or benefits that the parties to an economic exchange impose on those not involved in the exchange. Thus, a public good, which can be consumed by many people simultaneously, can be interpreted as

imposing external benefits on those who thereby consume it but do not pay for it. In the case of universal cheap mail delivery, the external benefit or externality to which mail delivery contributes is the vast, powerful, continental nation that increases the wealth and security of all its citizens.

2. Portions of this section draw on the article by Kuznets (1977).

3. Data in this section are drawn largely from Maddison (1998).

References

Aron, Leon. "The Strange Case of Russian Capitalism," *AEI Russian Outlook* (Washington: American Enterprise Institute for Public Policy Research, Winter 1998). Available on Internet at http://www.aei.org/ro/ro8906.htm.

Benham, Lee. "The Effect of Advertising on the Price of Eyeglasses," *Journal of Law and Economics*, vol. XV(2), October 1972, pp. 337-52.

Carson, Richard. *Comparative Economic Systems*, vol. II, 2nd edition (Armonk, N.Y.: M. E. Sharpe, 1997).

Denison, Edward F. *Accounting for United States Economic Growth 1929-1969* (Washington: The Brookings Institution, 1974).

Feldstein, Martin. "Russia's Rebirth," *Wall Street Journal*, September 8, 1997, p. A18.

Gregory, Paul R., and Robert C. Stuart. *Comparative Economic Systems*, 5th edition (Boston: Houghton Mifflin, 1995).

Katz, Lawrence F., Gary W. Loveman, and David G. Blanchflower. *A Comparison of Changes in the Structure of Wages in Four OECD Countries* (Chicago: University of Chicago Press, 1995).

Kohler, Heinz. "Soviet Central Planning," in David Kennett and Marc Lieberman, eds., *The Road to Capitalism* (Ft. Worth: Dryden Press, 1992), pp. 5-14.

Kornai, Janos. "The Soft Budget Constraint," *Kyklos*, vol. 39, fasc. 1, 1986, pp. 3-30.

Kroll, Heidi. "Monopoly and Transition to the Market," in David Kennett and Marc Lieberman, eds., *The Road to Capitalism* (Ft. Worth: Dryden Press, 1992), pp. 159-173.

Kuznets, Simon. "Two Centuries of Economic Growth: Reflections on U. S. Experience," *American Economic Review*, vol. 67(1), February 1977, pp. 1-14.

Lardy, Nicholas. "China's Unfinished Economic Transition," in Annette Brown, ed., *When Is Transition Over?* (Kalamazoo: W.E. Upjohn Institute, 1999), pp. 69-76.

Lipton, David, and Jeffrey Sachs. "The Consequences of Central Planning in Eastern Europe," in David Kennett and Marc Lieberman, eds., *The Road to Capitalism* (Ft. Worth: Dryden Press, 1992), pp. 27-36.

Litwack, John M. "Legality and Market Reform in Soviet-Type Economies," *Journal of Economic Perspectives*, vol. 5(4), Fall 1991, pp. 77-89.

Maddison, Angus. *Chinese Economic Performance in the Long Run* (Paris: Organisation for Economic Co-operation and Development, 1998).

Mankiw, N. Gregory. *Macroeconomics*, 4th edition (New York: Worth, 2000).

LESSON ONE
BROAD SOCIAL GOALS OF ECONOMIC SYSTEMS

INTRODUCTION

The same basic problem confronts different economic systems. How each nation deals with the fundamental economic problem of scarce resources and unlimited wants is determined by its economic system. All economic systems strive to achieve a set of broad social goals, usually including economic freedom, efficiency, equity, growth, and stability. How wisely these goals are chosen and assigned priorities, and how successful an economy is at achieving these goals through its laws, public policies, and system of economic incentives, determines how well it improves the quality of life for its citizens. Different nations and types of economic systems tend to value some goals more than others. At the beginning of the 21st century, however, more and more nations are moving away from command economies, and relying on market systems to allocate their scarce resources.

CONCEPTS

Broad social goals (efficiency, equity, freedom, growth, stability)
Command economy
Market economy

CONTENT STANDARDS

Different methods can be used to allocate goods and services. People, acting individually or collectively through government, must choose which methods to use to allocate different kinds of goods and services.

BENCHMARKS

There are essential differences between a market economy, in which allocations result from individuals making decisions as buyers and sellers, and a command economy, in which resources are allocated by a central authority.

OBJECTIVES

♦ Students explain how economic systems can be evaluated using broad social goals.

♦ Students evaluate the relative importance of the social goals in different economic systems.

♦ Students analyze data to determine the success of various countries in achieving their broad social goals and improving the quality of life of their citizens.

LESSON DESCRIPTION

Students create their own utopian society by rating five broad social goals. They learn about characteristics of command economies and market economies and make judgments about the goals that are most valued in each type of system. Finally, using data that measure various kinds of national economic performance, they evaluate the economic systems of different countries using the five social goals.

TIME REQUIRED

One to two class periods.

MATERIALS

- Activity 1: Broad Social Goals, one per student, and a visual
- Activity 2: Comparing Command and Market Economies, one per student
- Activity 3: Social Goal Achievement, one per student
- Activity 4: Economic Performance Indicators, one per student, and a visual

PROCEDURES

1. Explain to students that each economic system deals with the same basic economic problem: deciding how to use available resources to satisfy some of its citizens' wants

for goods and services, but knowing that it is impossible to satisfy all of those wants. The public policies that are implemented to address this basic economic problem in different nations will depend at least partly on the value or importance each nation assigns to a set of broad social goals. These goals are ultimately the criteria used to evaluate an economic system; but people in different nations and with different types of economic systems often disagree about which of these goals is most important.

2. Display a visual of Activity 1 and distribute copies to each student. Review the definitions for each goal and make the following points.

A. Total economic freedom is not possible. Some individual freedoms must be restricted to benefit the general welfare of society. For example, it is illegal to buy or sell some kinds of goods and services (such as heroin and votes), and the legal obligation to pay taxes restricts people's ability to decide how to spend some part of their incomes. The sale or purchase of other kinds of products is often partially restricted (such as the sale of alcohol and tobacco products to minors). All societies establish laws that sometimes enhance and sometimes restrict economic freedom.

B. Economic growth is measured by an increase in **real gross domestic product** (GDP), or the annual level of national income adjusted for inflation. **Real GDP per capita** is real GDP divided by a nation's population. This provides a basic measure of a country's standard of living. To increase GDP per capita while its population is growing or stable, a country must increase the number of goods and services produced each year. A target annual growth rate of 3 to 4 percent in real GDP is generally considered to be a reasonable and sustainable goal, as long as the economy

is investing in capital resources and the education and training of workers, and there is some level of technological progress. Economic growth is closely related to other broad social goals. For example, it can lead to more jobs and lower levels of unemployment, greater economic efficiency, and provide additional resources to assist low-income families to reduce poverty and promote greater equity. Higher rates of economic growth are sometimes not sustainable, and can result in inflation. When that happens, a nation may have to accept lower levels of growth for a time, in order to curb inflation.

C. When workers are unemployed for a month or a year the goods and services they could have produced during that period are lost forever. That means that countries with high unemployment rates are wasting some of their most important scarce resources. In market economies, however, not all unemployment is undesirable because workers are free to change jobs to find the most desirable jobs, workplaces, and places to live. In the U.S. economy today, this kind of **frictional unemployment** accounts for an unemployment rate of about 4-5%. Unemployment rates above this level represent a different and much more serious kind of problem in the economy, such as slowing or decreasing levels of total spending.

Inflation and **deflation** are changes (increases and decreases, respectively) in the average level of prices for the goods and services produced in the economy. Unexpected changes in the price level hurt some groups of people and help others. For example, unexpected inflation hurts people on fixed incomes and people who have loaned out money at fixed interest rates, but helps those who have borrowed money at fixed

From *Focus: Economic Systems*, © National Council on Economic Education, New York, NY

interest rates. When price levels are stable, people and businesses don't have to spend time and effort to look for ways to protect their incomes and investments from inflation or deflation. In other words, price stability improves both economic security and the overall climate for investment.

D. Economic equity concerns issues of fairness, and there are no economic or scientific procedures to prove that something is fair or unfair. Nevertheless, people's beliefs about what is right and wrong are extremely important in discussions about many kinds of public policies, such as the level and type of income-assistance programs for low-income families, and the rate at which people who earn different levels of income should be taxed to pay for government programs.

E. Economic efficiency means an economy is producing as much as possible to satisfy peoples' wants. The general rule economists use to decide whether it is efficient to make more of any kind of output is to compare the value of the additional benefits and costs entailed. If the additional benefits exceed the additional costs, it is efficient to do it. If the additional costs exceed the additional benefits, it is inefficient and should not be done.

3. Tell students that they now have an opportunity to create their own utopian society. Explain that each student has 100 points to allocate across these different broad social goals. Have students write the number of points they would allocate to each goal in the space provided on Activity 1. For example, if students value economic freedom more than any of the other goals, they would give it a higher number of points. If they place relatively little value on economic stability, they would assign it a smaller number of points. Make sure all students assign a total of 100 points.

4. Ask several students to tell how they distributed their 100 points and to explain their decisions. There will probably be a wide range of distributions. Ask students why this occurred. (*Students' values and preferences differ.*) Ask students if political leaders at the local and national level would likely show similar differences of opinion about these broad social goals. (*Members of different political parties, and even members of the same political party, regularly express different ideas about the relative importance of these kinds of goals. That explains a large part of their disagreements about spending priorities and tax reforms.*)

5. Tally the total number of points students in the class allocated for each goal and write that number on the visual next to each goal. Tell students this represents the utopian society preferred by the overall class. Explain that preferences of individual citizens may be different from those of a nation. An individual's support for an economic system depends largely on his or her acceptance of the nation's targeted economic goals. Save this information to use in the assessment activity.

6. Point out that just as individual students differ in how they value broad social goals, so too do supporters of different kinds of economic systems. Distribute copies of Activity 2. Have students read the descriptions of the two types of economic systems. Refer to the introductory essay by George Horwich to provide further background on each point. Discuss how each of the economic systems values the broad social goals:

A. Freedom (*Market: Individual freedom is highly valued, reflected by private ownership of most resources.* *Command: Government restricts individual freedom, with many decisions made by central planners and government ownership of most natural and capital resources.)*

B. Growth (*Market: Efficient use of resources results from individual and business incentives to produce more and avoid waste. Specialization and trade encourage higher levels of output. Investments in capital and workers' education and training promote future growth in productive capacity and output. Command: Central planners set growth targets and assign output quotas for different industries and firms. The production of consumer goods and services may be curtailed if planners want to focus on other sectors (e.g., military). Incentives to reduce waste are weak. Plant and equipment maintenance are often significant problems.)*

C. Stability (*Market: The federal government conducts monetary policies – in the United States, through the Federal Reserve System – and uses fiscal policies to promote full employment (the 4-5 percent unemployment rates in the United States reflect frictional unemployment). Command: Planners set prices thus controlling official measures of inflation, although shortages can make effective prices significantly higher than the prices set by planners. If high employment is a key goal, virtually no unemployment – even frictional unemployment from workers changing jobs – will be accepted. Higher employment may be achieved through high labor/capital ratios, which can reduce productivity, efficiency, and growth.)*

D. Equity (*Market: Evaluation of equity is based more on voluntary exchange and equality of opportunity rather than equality of outcomes. Income depends on the value of labor and other resources an individual has to sell.*

Some U.S. government spending and tax programs provide modest redistribution of income, but less so than in most other Western market economies. Command: Wages can be set by government to provide greater equality of income, which some view as more equitable. V.I. Lenin and other communist leaders often claimed that they were eliminating the capitalist "exploitation" of labor. In practice, many command economies have substantial income inequality, because of high salaries and other forms of compensation for key government or political party officials, and other selected professionals such as military leaders and "star" athletes. Even if official salaries are low, better housing and other services make real incomes higher for these groups.)

E. Efficiency (*Market: Most allocation decisions are made by consumers and private firms in markets. Extensive specialization and international trade increase productivity and competition. Firms and consumers promote their self-interest by taking actions whenever additional benefits exceed additional costs. Command: Allocation decisions are made by central planners, with few or no effective market signals and incentives. A focus on eliminating unemployment can lead to inefficient mixes of labor and capital resources. State-owned enterprises that are inefficient are rarely, if ever, allowed to fail.)*

7. Distribute Activity 3. Ask students to rate how effective they think each country's economic system is in achieving each broad social goal by using a rating scale of 1 (poor) to 5 (excellent). Discuss the following questions:

A. Which social goals receive the greatest emphasis in a command economy? (*Equality of outcome but not*

From *Focus: Economic Systems,* © National Council on Economic Education, New York, NY

opportunity, stability, and growth as determined in production goals set by central planners.)

B. Which goals are most important in a market economy? (*Freedom, efficiency, growth, equality of opportunity but not outcome.*)

8. Distribute a copy of Activity 4 to each student and display a visual of Activity 4. Explain to students that the degree to which social goals have been achieved can be measured, up to a point, by using certain data. Review the various indicators that are used and their definitions. Some indicators may need explanation:

A. **Gross National Product** (GNP) is the total market value of all final goods and services produced by a country in one year. (The final product of bread includes such intermediate products as flour and milk. The value of these inputs is already included in the value of the final product, bread, so only the price of the bread is counted in GNP, not the price of the bread plus the price of the inputs used to make the bread.)

B. GNP PPP is gross national product data for several countries converted to a common currency (dollars), based on exchange rates for the different national currencies that reflect **purchasing power parity** (PPP). PPP exchange rates determine the equivalent values for two currencies by considering prices for all goods and services in the two nations. This differs from exchange rates that are determined only by the prices for imports and exports, which are reported every day in the financial press.

C. The **GDP Implicit deflator** measures the average annual rate of price changes in a nation's economy.

D. The **Gini index** measures the degree of income equality for the distribution of income (or in some cases consumption expenditures) across individuals or households in an economy. A Gini index of zero indicates perfect equality, where each person or household has the same income. A Gini index of 100 indicates perfect inequality, which would mean that the richest person or household in the country received all of the income, and all other people or households received nothing. (See Lesson 12 in this volume for more on Gini measures of equality.)

E. The Index of Economic Freedom is a ranking of the world's economies on 10 broad categories: banking, capital flows and foreign investment, monetary policy, fiscal burden of the government, wages and prices, trade policy, government intervention in the economy, property rights, regulation, and black markets. The lower the index score, the higher the degree of economic freedom in the country. The data for this entry in Activity 4 are for 2000.

9. Discuss:

A. Which country has the most economic freedom? (*United States*) The least? (*India*)

B. Which country has the highest GNP PPP and GNP PPP/capita? (*United States*) the lowest? (*India*) Which country has the highest standard of living? (*United States*) The lowest? (*India*)

C. Which countries had the greatest economic stability – low unemployment and stable prices? (*United States and Japan*) The least stability? (*Russia*) Why is Germany's unemployment rate so high? (*After the unification of East and West Germany, many former East*

Germans lost their jobs when the government-owned factories in which they were employed could not compete and were closed. Also, higher unemployment rates are common across Western Europe because of wage regulations related to government policies such as unemployment insurance.)

D. What does the Gini index tell you about income distribution in these countries? (*The United States, China, and Russia have the least income equality.*)

E. What generalization can be made from these data about the level of economic freedom in a country and the general welfare of its citizens? (*Countries with high degrees of economic freedom have higher rates of GNP and economic growth, and their citizens appear to enjoy higher standards of living. These countries also tend to have low unemployment, stable prices, and high literacy rates.*)

10. Using the information from Activity 4, instruct students to reevaluate their ratings for each country on Activity 3. Cross out any old ratings that change and record the new ratings.

11. Discuss:

A. Why does the United States score so high and India so low? (*The broad social goals can be used as criteria to judge how well an economy is doing. The U.S. fares well on all the criteria; India does not.*) What could be some reasons why India fares so poorly? (*High incidence of poverty, high levels of government regulation and control.*)

B. Ask students how their ratings were similar to or different from the actual performance of the countries. Why do

they think this occurred? (*Answers will vary.*)

C. Point out that no economic system is a pure command or a pure market economy, but some have more market or command characteristics than others. Ask students to rate the countries from most market oriented to least.

CLOSURE

1. What are the basic social goals that can be used to evaluate an economy? (*Efficiency, equity, growth, freedom and stability.*)

2. Review the definitions of the social goals. (*See Activity 1.*)

3. Describe how a command economy and a market economy value the broad social goals. (*People and political leaders in all types of economic systems are likely to view all of the goals as important, but there are some general differences to be noted. Command economies tend to value stability and equality of outcome more than market economies. Central planners set prices, output quotas, capital and investment allocations, and sometimes even wages to insure that everyone is employed. The emphasis on growth is determined by central planners. Economic freedom is sacrificed to achieve goals that planners determine are best for the general welfare of society. Market economies tend to stress freedom, efficiency, and growth, and equality of opportunity more than equality of outcome.*)

4. How well are the broad social goals met by alternative economic systems? (*Countries that are more market oriented tend to perform better than centrally planned command economies on a wide range of outcomes.*)

5. Why are so many countries in the world moving toward a more market-oriented economy? (*Market economies tend to have high levels of economic freedom, growth, and income, and do reasonably well in terms of*

*stability as well. Though often debated, many
people believe that market economies are also
preferred to command economies on the basis of
equity, particularly in terms of equality of
opportunity.)*

ASSESSMENT

1. Instruct students to return to Activity 1.
Display the visual of Activity 1. Write the
following on the board:

"Using *either* your individual *or* the class
rankings for the social goals, determine if the
utopian society would likely be more market or
command oriented, and justify your answer. Be
sure to predict how the economy would fare on
each of the social goals, and discuss what that
would mean for the citizens of this nation."

Activity 1
Broad Social Goals

_____ **Economic Freedom** refers to such things as the freedom for consumers to decide how to spend or save their incomes, for workers to change jobs or join unions, and for people to establish new businesses or close old ones.

_____ **Economic Growth** refers to increasing the production of goods and services over time. The rate of economic growth is measured by changes in the level of real gross domestic product (GDP) or real gross national product (GNP).

_____ **Economic Stability** refers to stable prices and full employment. Price stability means avoiding inflation, a rise in the average price level, or deflation, a fall in the average price level. Full employment means using all of an economy's scarce resources, particularly labor.

_____ **Economic Equity** refers to concerns about fairness in economic dealings. These concerns usually arise in evaluating exchanges, or the overall distribution of income. Some people judge equity based on providing equal opportunity, others based on the equality of outcomes. Public policies are often evaluated in terms of what people think is right or wrong, even though people often disagree about what is fair or unfair.

_____ **Economic Efficiency** means not wasting scarce resources. For a national economy that entails two things: 1) producing the goods and services people want most, and 2) economizing resources in the production of goods and services, so that the real costs of production are as low as possible.

From _Focus: Economic Systems_, © National Council on Economic Education, New York, NY

Activity 2
Comparing Command and Market Economies

In Command Economies	In Market Economies
Government ownership of all nonhuman resources	Private ownership of all types of resources
Primary allocation of resources determined by central planners	Market prices direct products and resources
Income equality promoted by wages that are set by planners. Zero unemployment. State enterprises never fail because of government subsidies, permission to raise prices, or exemption from tax liabilities.	Income depends on the resources an individual has to sell. Some forms of unemployment are tolerated because of people changing jobs, changes in skills sought by employers, cyclical fluctuations, and seasonal changes in demand.
Central planners make production decisions to meet social goals, with limited consideration of consumer preferences. Consumers have no influence on price, quantity or quality of products produced.	Consumer demand is the driving force behind firms' production decisions.
Limited foreign trade to maintain economic independence	International specialization promotes competition and holds production costs and prices down
Prices usually set below the market clearing price ensure that goods are sold and control officially measured inflation.	Prices adjust to keep consumption and production at market equilibrium levels.

Activity 3
Social Goal Achievement

Evaluate how successful you believe each country has been in achieving the social goals listed. Rate each country on each goal using a scale of 1 (poor) to 5 (excellent).

Goal	China	Germany	India	Japan	U.S.	Russia
Freedom						
Growth						
Stability						
Equity						
Efficiency						
Overall Rating						

From *Focus: Economic Systems*, © National Council on Economic Education, New York, NY

Activity 4
Economic Performance Indicators

Indicator	China	Germany	India	Japan	U.S.	Russia
GNP PPP $ (billions) 1998	3,983.6	1,708.5	1,660.9	2,928.4	7,922.6	579.8
GNP PPP/capita $ 1998	3,220	20,810	1,700	23,180	29,340	3,950
GNP/capita 1997-1998 average annual percent growth rate	6.5	-0.4	4.2	-2.8	2.8	-6.3
GDP implicit deflator 1990-1998	9.8	2.2	7.5	0.4	2.2	235.3
Index of Economic Freedom 2000[a]	3.4	2.20	3.80	2.15	1.80	3.70
Unemployment rate 1998 est.	3%[b]	10.6%	NA	4.4%	4.5%	11.5%[c]
Infant mortality /1000 live births 1998	32	5	70	4	7	17
Percentage 15 and older who read and write	81.5	99	52	99	97	98
Gini index 1999	45	28.1	29.7	24.9 (1995)	40.1	48 (1994)
Foreign Trade as percentage of GDP PPP 1998	8.3	55	3.9	21.3	19.9	14
Central Govt. revenue as percentage of GDP 1998	4.8	31	12	20.9 (GNP 1995)	21.9	17.9 (1997)
Percentage existing on less than $2 PPP/day	57.8 (1995)	...	87.5 (1994)	...	...	10.9

Sources: The World Factbook 1999, Central Intelligence Agency; 2000 World Development Indicators, The World Bank; Entering the 21st Century World Development Report 1999/2000, The World Bank.
[a]Source: 2000 Index of Economic Freedom, The Heritage Foundation and the Wall Street Journal.
[b]Officially 3 percent urban, probably 8-10 percent because of substantial unemployment and underemployment in rural areas.
[c]Considerable underemployment

LESSON TWO
WHO DECIDES?

INTRODUCTION

All economies face the same fundamental problem of **scarcity** – limited resources versus unlimited wants. How a nation allocates its resources to satisfy some wants using its human, natural, and capital resources depends upon the type of economic system it uses. Command economies generally have a group of central planners who make allocation decisions designed to satisfy goals adopted by the central planners themselves, or goals assigned to them by the country's political leaders. In market economies consumer sovereignty directs resource allocation for the production of most goods and services. Consumers spend their dollars, in effect voting to indicate preferences for goods and services. Producers compete for the dollars that consumers spend, and use information about these spending patterns and production costs to make production and pricing decisions for the particular goods they decide to offer for sale in the marketplace.

CONCEPTS

Resource allocation
Market economy
Command economy

CONTENT STANDARDS

Different methods can be used to allocate goods and services. People, acting individually or collectively through government, must choose which methods to use to allocate different kinds of goods and services.

BENCHMARKS

People in all economies must answer three basic economic questions: What goods and services will be produced? How will these goods and services be produced? Who will consume them?

Comparing the benefits and costs of different allocation methods in order to choose the method that is most appropriate for some specific problem can result in more effective allocations and a more effective allocation system.

OBJECTIVES

♦ Students describe how command and market economies answer the basic economic questions of what to produce, how to produce it, and for whom.

♦ Students explain the effects of using different procedures to make resource allocation decisions in command and market economies.

LESSON DESCRIPTION

Working in groups students determine how command and market economies use different procedures to make resource allocation decisions. With this information, students explore how both types of economies might respond to various events that are presented as newspaper headlines.

TIME REQUIRED

One or two class periods.

MATERIALS

- Visual 1: The Economic Problem
- Visual 2: Census Data Report
- Visual 3: How Command and Market Economies Answer Basic Economic Questions
- Activity 1: Characteristics of Country A's Economy, one per student
- Activity 2: Characteristics of Country B's Economy, one per student
- Activity 3: News Events, 2 copies cut apart
- Activity 4: Assessment, one per student

PROCEDURES

1. Display Visual 1. Tell students that *all* economies face the same fundamental economic problem: human wants for goods and services

greatly exceed what can be produced using all available productive resources—natural, human and capital. This imbalance of wants and resources requires people in any kind of economic system to answer hard questions about how to use their resources to satisfy some, but not all, wants. There are three basic questions that every economic system must answer:

   A. What goods and services will be produced?
   B. How will goods and services be produced?
   C. For whom will these goods and services be produced?

2. Discuss each of the three basic questions with the class, to bring out some of the key ideas encompassed in each question. Specifically, point out that the What question entails deciding how much of each good or service will be produced; the How question entails deciding what production methods and mix of resources will be used to produce different goods and services; and the For Whom question involves decisions about which households and individuals will receive goods and services to consume or use in other ways.

3. Explain that the institutions and methods a country uses to answer these three basic questions determine the kind of economic system that exists in the country. In recent centuries, there have been two major types of economic systems, command and market economies.

4. Divide students into groups of four. Provide half of the groups with copies of Activity 1 and half with copies of Activity 2.

5. Display Visual 2 and read it to the class. Instruct the groups to use the information from Activity 1 or 2 to determine how their economy will respond. Have groups discuss what changes will be made (if any) in the goods and services produced, and how these teenagers will

be prepared to enter the workforce of their country.

6. Ask each group to tell how their economy responded to the information about a growing population of teenagers and explain why. (*Country A's response: Because central planners determine how resources are allocated, they will only respond to the information to a degree that is consistent with their overall goals. Here, the central planning groups were not assigned a set of goals. Some of the groups may have determined goals explicitly, others only implicitly as reflected in their responses to the events.* (See Lesson 1 for more on the most common economic goals adopted by command and market economies. It is unlikely that all of the central planning groups adopted the same goals, and that is an important general point to make.) *In this particular situation, it is quite possible that the wants of a growing number of young consumers will have little effect on the overall production goals. That might be even more likely if the central planners were not high school students, but rather much older people. Country B's response: As demand for goods and services frequently purchased by teenagers. increases, the prices for these goods will increase. Increased prices will encourage greater production of these products by current producers of these products, and possibly by new producers as well. As a result, more resources will be allocated to the production of goods and services demanded by teenagers.*) Similar kinds of differences will be noted in the process of preparing the teenagers for the workforce.

7. In general, how are answers to the What, How, and For Whom questions determined in Country A? (*By central planners, who may or may not have placed great weight on consumer preferences.*) In Country B? (*By individual consumers who purchase the things they want most and can afford with their income, and by individual producers seeking higher profits.*)

8. Summarize the discussion by explaining that Country A has a command economy and Country B has a market economy.

9. Display Visual 3. Review the general characteristics of each type of economy using the questions below. Record responses under column 1 for Command Economy and column 2 for Market Economy.

A. How did your country determine what to produce? (**Command**: *Central planners base production on politically determined goals.* **Market**: *Consumer preferences (demand) and producer cost and profit considerations (supply) determine what to produce.* How does your country determine how much of a good to produce? (*Same as above.*)

B. How does your country determine how the goods and services will be produced? (**Command**: *Central planners determine the combination of productive resources used based on the country's goals (e.g., using more labor and less capital if employment is a major goal).* **Market**: *Individual businesses determine the mix of natural, human, and capital resources they will use to minimize production costs and maximize profits.*)

C. Who receives the goods and services produced? (**Command**: *Wages and other incomes are set by central planners, as are prices for goods and services consumers can buy. Those prices are often set below market clearing price levels, creating shortages. When that happens, consumers who are willing and able to spend time searching for goods, or standing in long lines, will get the products. Or consumers may offer to do special favors for those who sell the goods, or offer bribes or higher money prices, even though that is illegal.* **Market**: *The value of a good or service is the price determined by the interactions of buyers and sellers in the marketplace. Goods and services are purchased by buyers (who may be consumers, or businesses, or government agencies) willing and able to pay the market price. Consumers reflect their preferences for goods and services through dollar votes. Producers compete for the dollars that consumers spend, and use information about spending patterns and their own production costs to make production and pricing decisions for the goods they decide to sell.*)

10. Distribute additional copies of Activity 1 and 2 so each student has a copy of both. Instruct students to label Activity 1 as Command Economy and Activity 2 as Market Economy.

11. Divide students into new groups of 3 or 4, mixing students from the original groups, so that each group now has at least one student who was originally in a command economy group, and at least one who was in a market economy group. Provide each group with one of the news events from Activity 3. Make sure more than one group is working on each of the events.

12. Tell the groups they should discuss resource allocation responses to the problem in their news event from either a command or market perspective, or a combination of both. Inform groups they will report their decisions by reading the assigned news event, then indicating how their economy would respond, and explaining why they believe this is the best solution. The other groups will discuss whether the proposed solution represents a command or market-based solution, or some combination of both, and explain their answers. If a proposed solution is determined to be a combination of command and market policies, students should identify which basic economic questions were answered from a command perspective and which from a market perspective. For example,

a group may choose to answer the what to produce question using a central planning approach, but rely on the market to determine who will get the goods and services that are produced.

13. The answers below provide a response for each news event in Activity 3 from both command and market perspectives. Students may use a combination of both.

A. *Command: Production and distribution of goods and services for disaster relief is directed by government agencies. Market: Prices rise for relief and repair goods and services in afflicted areas. Private businesses would respond by sending supplies. Nonprofit agencies funded by private donations may also send supplies and people to help.*

B. *Command: Central planners determine how many resources are allocated to hospital construction, production of supplies, and education of medical personnel. The planners weigh the tradeoff between the cost of providing more medical services and the length of time people must wait for the services. Market: Prices for medical services will rise as long as people want more services than are available at current prices. Private firms and nonprofit agencies respond by building more hospitals. Rising salaries will attract more people to careers in health care. Those not willing and able to pay higher prices for these services, or higher premiums for insurance policies for health care services, will do without or rely on clinics operated by charitable organizations.*

C. *Command: Central planners could determine that more individuals should go into teaching, or allow class sizes to increase, or some combination of the two. Market: Salaries for teachers would rise, and some districts might pay bonuses for new teachers, especially in geographic areas and academic fields where shortages are most severe.*

D. *Command: Most likely nothing would change unless the production of goods related to hot weather and the control of global warming were part of the central planners' overall goals. Market: The demand for fans, air conditioners, lightweight clothing and related goods would rise, and the demand for winter items would probably decrease. But possible causes of the global warming, such as pollutants associated with automobile emissions, will likely not be addressed in private markets.* (See Lessons 3, 6, and 11 for a discussion of environmental issues and other "market failures." You may also want to discuss the idea that, to the extent that this is truly a global problem, some sort of international agreements may be required to solve the problem, regardless of whether national economies are market or command.)

E. *Command: Central planners will probably not recognize the demand for faddish items. That means they may not allocate resources to the production of either toy. But if their plans reflect last year's demand for toys, they are likely to produce too many of the old toys, and too few of the new ones, compared to this year's demand for both toys. Market: Prices and production levels would fall sharply for last year's toy and increase sharply for the new toy.* Note that if these toys are patented or trademarked they may only be sold by one producer, although other producers are likely to rush to produce "imitations" or "improved" versions of the new toy.

CLOSURE

Review with students how command and market economies allocate resources. Discuss the following:

1. What basic questions must every economy answer because of the fundamental economic problem of scarcity? *(What – and how much – to produce, how to produce goods and services, and for whom to produce them?)*

2. How are the basic economic questions answered in a command economy? *(A central authority or group of planners establish goals and allocate resources to try to achieve those goals. The central planners determine what is produced, the mix of resources used to produce the goods and services, and prices for goods and services, which are often set below the market price, resulting in shortages. Consumers who buy the goods and services at the fixed prices frequently stand in long lines waiting to make purchases, and spend time searching for stores where goods and services are for sale. They may also offer special services or higher prices – i.e., bribes – to sellers.)*

3. How are the basic economic questions answered in a market economy? *(Most resources are privately owned, and how these resources are used is determined in the marketplace. Consumers indicate their preferences for goods and services through dollar votes. Producers then determine the amount of goods and services to produce and how they will produce them. They decide how much to supply by comparing the cost of producing the product to the price they expect to receive for it.)*

ASSESSMENT

1. Distribute a copy of Activity 4 to each student.

2. Instruct students to read the situation and complete the question. *(Suggested answer: The cafeteria manager and principal are serving as the central planning group for the cafeteria. They make decisions on what should be produced, how it should be produced, and perhaps even the price for the lunches. The market rewrite should make reference to the cafeteria offering food choices based on student preferences, at prices competitive with private food outlets. Students might even suggest bringing in one or more private food companies to run the cafeteria, or replacing the cafeteria with a food mall featuring commercial food products. Students should provide the advantages and disadvantages of their proposals.)*

Visual 1
The Economic Problem

1. Choices must be made in all economic systems because:
    - **Resources (natural, human, and capital) are limited or scarce.**
    - **Human wants are unlimited.**

2. Using resources one way, to satisfy some wants, means those resources cannot be used in other ways, to satisfy other wants.

3. Every economic system must answer three basic economic questions:
    - **What and how much to produce?**
    - **How to produce?**
    - **For Whom to produce?**

4. How the basic economic questions are answered in a country determines the type of economic system (usually market, command, or some mix).

 From *Focus: Economic Systems*, © National Council on Economic Education, New York, NY

Visual 2
Census Data Report

Number of Teenagers Increases

- Demographic studies indicate that over the next five years the number of teenagers, especially ages 15-18, will increase dramatically.

- The greater number of teenagers is expected to affect many products and groups including:
  - schools
  - teachers
  - clothing
  - entertainment
  - transportation
  - fast food
  - jobs
  - college enrollment

Visual 3
How Command and Market Economies Answer Basic Economic Questions

Command	Basic Questions	Market
	What and How Much to Produce?	
	How to Produce?	
	For Whom to Produce?	

From *Focus: Economic Systems*, © National Council on Economic Education, New York, NY

Activity 1
Characteristics of Country A's Economy

- **Except for human resources, the government or state owns most productive resources.**

- **Central planners determine what goods and services will be produced and how much of each will be produced.**

- **Central planners try to achieve goals they establish, or that are established by political leaders.**

- **Prices for goods and services are set by central planners, often below market clearing price levels. This creates shortages.**

Activity 2
Characteristics of Country B's Economy

- **Productive resources are privately owned and controlled by individuals.**

- **Prices determined in markets for goods and services, and in markets for labor and other productive resources, largely determine how resources are allocated.**

- **Consumers show their preferences for goods and services with dollar votes. Producers respond by comparing the cost of producing different products to the prices they expect to receive from consumers.**

- **Buyers and sellers are motivated by self-interest.**

Activity 3
News Events

1. Floods and mudslides blanket the coast. Hurricane-force winds destroy homes. People are without food, shelter, and power.
2. Health Care Crisis: Country is plagued by shortages of hospital rooms, equipment, doctors, and nurses. Hundreds of citizens wait months for heart surgery and cancer treatment.
3. Mass teacher shortage nears. Fifty percent of state's teachers are eligible for retirement in next five years.
4. Global warming is here. Latest federal report says temperatures rising. Sixteen of the last 20 years exceeded the annual average since 1895. Summer expected to be hottest on record.
5. Last year's hard-to-find, hot new toy sits on shelves this holiday season. This year, the Millennium Bear® tops wish list for kids and adults.

Activity 4
Assessment

Directions: Read the scenario below and complete the task that follows.

At Hometown High School the cafeteria manager and the principal determine what foods will be sold in the cafeteria. They select foods they feel are healthy for the students. Their goal is to provide nutritional meals using government-subsidized products. To insure that all students can afford lunch, they sell the meals at a very low price.

Preferences of students fall on deaf ears. The manager and principal refuse to change the menu because students want foods they find unacceptable. Students are staging a silent protest by bringing lunches from home, filled with the foods they like.

Task:

Explain how running the school cafeteria is similar to running a command economy. Rewrite the scenario to show how the cafeteria might be run more like a private business in a market economy. Then discuss the major advantages and disadvantages of each way of running the cafeteria.

LESSON THREE
PROPERTY RIGHTS, THE TRAGEDY OF THE COMMONS, AND THE COASE THEOREM

INTRODUCTION

Property rights, standards for conducting business (including liability laws), and government enforcement of these laws and standards establish the basic rules and incentives that individuals and firms face in making economic decisions about consumption, investments and production. Without these incentives, much less investment and risk-taking would be undertaken in the economy.

Economists who support market systems as the most effective and equitable way to allocate resources have long noted the key role of property rights. But economists who favor central planning, such as Karl Marx, have called for the end of private property. During the last century many attempts were made to develop modern industrial economies without the linchpin of private property, but most eventually failed. The absence of property rights seems to have played a key role in those failures.

When property is owned publicly, rather than privately, it is often overused and abused. This problem was noted in 1832 by the economist William Forster Lloyd, who was concerned about overgrazing on public pasture land in England. Acknowledging the inevitability of these problems, the biologist Garrett Hardin coined the now familiar phrase, "the tragedy of the commons," in 1968.

In 1960, economist Ronald Coase argued that when negotiating costs are small and property rights are well defined, the efficient outcome or solution to disputes about how

resources might be used will be reached by the parties involved in the dispute, without government intervention, regardless of which party is assigned the right to use land or other property as they want. This important contribution earned Coase the Nobel Prize in Economics in 1992.

This lesson demonstrates the role of private property in establishing economic incentives, and in explaining the tragedy of the commons and the Coase theorem.

CONCEPTS

Property rights
Tragedy of the commons
Coase theorem

CONTENT STANDARDS

Institutions evolve in market economies to help individuals and groups accomplish their goals. Banks, labor unions, corporations, legal systems, and not-for-profit organizations are examples of important institutions. A different kind of institution, clearly defined and well enforced property rights, is essential to a market economy.

BENCHMARKS

Property rights, contract enforcement, standards for weights and measures, and liability rules affect incentives for people to produce and exchange goods and services.

OBJECTIVES

♦ Students identify how the assignment of property rights affects economic decision-making.

♦ Students verify, using numerical examples, that efficient outcomes are achieved without government intervention when the conditions of the Coase theorem apply.

♦ Students analyze the causes and consequences of a tragedy of the commons situation, using numerical examples.

LESSON DESCRIPTION

Students participate in simulations of a collective farm and an equal-shares society. Then they use simple numerical examples to demonstrate the relationship between collective ownership and the tragedy of the commons. Finally, they analyze a case of financial damages to see that when property rights are clear and the costs of buying and selling are low, efficient outcomes will be achieved, regardless of who is assigned property rights or the legal liability for damages to someone else's property.

TIME REQUIRED

Two class periods.

MATERIALS

- Visual 1: Keeping Them Down on the Collective Farm
- Visual 2: Property Rights, The Tragedy of the Commons, and the Coase Theorem in Market and Command Economies
- Activity 1: Keeping Them Down on the Collective Farm, one copy and one crayon for each student
- Activity 2: Share and Share Alike, one copy for each student
- Activity 3: Home in the Cupboard or Home on the Range: A Commons Tragedy, one copy for each student
- Activity 4: The Coase Theorem, one copy for each student
- Activity 5: Extension Exercise, one copy for each student
- Blank transparency sheet (optional).

PROCEDURES

1. Give each student a copy of Activity 1 and a crayon. Explain that in this activity they will take the role of peasant farmers working on a collective farm, in a simulation that has three rounds. Students will simulate the production of nutras and/or vitas by coloring the units on the handout.

2. Explain that in Round 1, they will be paid 10 Bucko$ for producing 10 nutras. They will "starve" if they produce less than 10 nutras, but will not be paid more than 10 Bucko$ if they produce more than 10. Tell the students to work only in the Round 1 section of the worksheet.

3. Conduct Round 1. Allow enough time (about a minute or two) for the average student to produce 10 nutras before stopping the production. Tell students to enter their yields and earnings in the blanks. Be sure to note exactly how much time you allowed for this round, and allow the same amount of time in the next two rounds.

4. Conduct Rounds 2 and 3, explaining the different payment schedules for each round as noted on the activity sheets. Record the harvest production of nutras and vitas and the amount of payments to all farmers after each round. Display the results on an overhead transparency, using Visual 1.

5. In the debriefing, ask: Did farmers produce as much as they could in each round? Why or why not? *(In Rounds 2 and 3 the incentives of private reward or ownership led to increased output and income.)*

6. Give each student a copy of Activity 2. Tell them that in this activity they are members of a communal society where all output produced is shared equally. Their goal is to maximize their own units of happiness (utility). In this activity, those units are obtained from NUBs (the output that is shared equally) **and** from leisure time.

7. Explain that the simulation is played in four rounds. In the first three rounds, emphasize that the total NUB output is shared by all, regardless of whether an individual makes a contribution to NUB production or not.

8. In each round, once students have selected the combination of hours devoted to work and leisure, have them enter the numbers

in columns (1) and (2) and report the work hours to you. This total represents the number of NUBs produced, which will be equally shared by all students. Announce this total to the class, along with the number of students present. Divide the NUBs by the number of students to determine the equal share received by each student. Instruct students to record this number in Column (4) of their worksheets. Then they should calculate how many units of happiness they have in this round by adding their hours of leisure and multiplying their units of NUB by two. Repeat these steps for Rounds 2 and 3.

9. Although the rules in the first three rounds do not change, it is likely that the first round will have the greatest production of NUBs. In later rounds, NUB production will probably decrease as students become dissatisfied with their share of the communal output. To demonstrate this pattern to students, record the results from each round and display them on an overhead transparency or on the board. Discuss the incentive problems of communal ownership and equal-share plans. Point out that over time many students are likely to "free ride" on the efforts and production of other students. That reduces the overall level of production, consumption, and the standard of living.

10. At the beginning of Round 4, announce that students will now be allowed to keep any NUBs that they produce. More students will choose to work all 10 hours, because each hour generates a NUB worth 2 units of happiness (utils) compared with one unit for an hour of leisure, and the NUBs produced are not shared with others. That eliminates the free-rider problem.

11. Give each student a copy of Activity 3. Read the short nursery rhyme, and ask students to keep the rhyme in mind when they analyze the Mrs. Hubbard problem in Part A. Have students answer these questions individually or in small groups.

Based on the nursery rhyme, how did the children behave with these common ownership rules for food? (*Because initially there are no individual property rights, the food tends to be consumed faster.*) Do you think each child ate two cinnamon rolls? (*It is unlikely that each child ate two rolls. The older, larger, or more aggressive children probably ate more. Anyone raised with siblings is familiar with the communal attitudes: "get it before someone else does" and "you snooze....you lose".*) How are the children likely to behave under the new rules? (*After Mrs. Hubbard assigns property rights to the treats, they usually last longer. However, respect for the newly defined property rights depends on Mrs. Hubbard's reputation as an enforcer of rules. If she doesn't enforce the rules, property rights will be ignored because the probability of punishment is low.*) Emphasize that the different responses stem from differences in the incentive systems associated with common vs. individual ownership rules, or property rights. The overuse of communally owned property, sometimes called the "tragedy of the commons," often results when resources are collectively or publicly owned.

12. Have students complete the questions in the extension exercise from Activity 3. Which is more likely to remain clean, a public restroom or a bathroom in your home or apartment? Why? (*The likelihood of using the same public bathroom in the near future is low, so its cleanliness is of less concern to most people who use it.*) Which is more likely to be well maintained, the outside grounds or interior living areas of an apartment complex? Does it matter if the apartments are condominiums (owned by the people who live in them), or they are all owned by one private owner, or owned by the government? Why? (*Privately owned living spaces are usually better maintained because they are assets owned by households. Therefore, the current and future values for those assets have a direct impact on families' wealth and standards of living. Commons areas*

are not as well maintained because of free-rider problems.)

13. Part B of Activity 3 describes a situation in which the collective ownership of the means of production leads to a tragedy of the commons. Students may find the analysis quite challenging, so have them read it and answer the questions as a class activity.

Round 1. Based on this information, how many residents will buy broods and how many will buy bonds? *(In Part B of Activity 3, the first allocation is three broods and seven bonds. Each of the 3 chicken investors earns $111 at the end of the period. No one will invest in the 4th chicken brood because it earns $5 less than the bond return of $110. Total income = (3 x $111) + (7 x $110) = $1,103.)*

Round 2. Now suppose the community elects one person to determine how to invest all of the money from the community in order to maximize the total investment income for the community. How many bonds and broods would be purchased? *(Two broods and eight bonds. The investment in the third brood was best for a private investor, yielding $111, **but** it adds only $101 to the community's income (the difference between $333 and $232). The opportunity cost of that resident's chicken investment is the income foregone in the bond market of $110. Total market income rises in the community by $9 if the investment in the third brood is switched to investing in another bond. This numerical example demonstrates the "tragedy of the commons". Maximizing individual returns in Round 1 led to an overuse of the commons, which reduced returns to other investors who were also using the commonly owned range.)*

Round 3. Suppose the common feeding area is sold to a single private owner who will raise chickens. How many broods of chickens will that person raise in each investment period? *(Privatizing the commons ends the incentive to overgraze. The private owner will now raise*

only two broods, because he or she bears all of the costs of the lower broodweights from grazing more broods. Note that the same brood result occurs in Rounds 2 and 3.)

14. Distribute one copy of Activity 4 to each student. Explain the conditions necessary for the Coase theorem to apply and discuss the important role of incentives in influencing economic behavior. Alert students that the same efficient outcome is predicted to occur no matter who has the property rights. Although the assignment of property rights does not affect the outcome, it does affect the distribution of income of the parties involved in the dispute.

Ask: If laws in this city favor Mochabucks, so that Megadent is legally responsible for these damages to Mochabucks' profits, what could Megadent do to keep Mochabucks' owner happy? *(If Mochabucks has the property rights, it can demand to be compensated. It is cheaper for Megadent to pay Mochabucks $400 rather than stop the damage and lose $1,000. Outcome: Mochabucks serves no customers; Megadent stays in business. Distributional consequences: Mochabucks receives $400; Megadent keeps $600 after paying damages. Total profits for the two firms are $1,000, or $600 higher than when only Mochabucks was operating.)*

Would Megadent go out of business? *(No. It still earns profits, although they are lower.)*

Now suppose the property rights to operate a business favor Megadent, and Mochabucks is not legally entitled to any damages from Megadent. What will happen in this case? *(If Megadent has the property rights to operate, it will refuse to compensate Mochabucks. Outcome: Mochabucks serves no customers; Megadent stays in business. Distributional consequences: Mochabucks receives $0; Megadent earns $1,000. Total profits are $1,000 or $600 higher than when just Mochabucks was operating. The outcomes are identical in terms of total profits and business* activity. *Mochabucks would prefer the first assignment of property rights, but Megadent prefers the second.)*

15. Assign the Activity 5 extension exercise as a writing assignment or a small group discussion. In this activity, students focus on the conditions necessary for the Coase theorem to hold, rather than assuming the Coase theorem always works. In theory, with fewer firms and stronger government power, a command economy might have advantages in dealing with pollution problems. However, historically the command economies have worse environmental records than the wealthier market economies. That partly reflects lower income levels in the command economies, which led central planners to put more weight on increasing production and income levels rather than environmental quality. But the absence of signals from consumers and voters concerning their demand for clean air and water also appears to have played a key role in the higher level of pollution in the former Soviet Union.

CLOSURE

1. Display Visual 2, and ask the class to discuss each of the questions listed there: How are property rights typically defined and enforced in market and command economies? (*Private property is a basic institution of market economies, so property rights are typically more extensive, more clearly defined, and better enforced by the legal system in a market economy.*) Would you expect to see more examples of "the tragedy of the commons" in market or command economies? Why? (*Much more property is commonly owned in command economies, so there will normally be more tragedy-of-the-commons problems in those systems than in market systems.*) Would the Coase theorem resolve all cases of economic damages imposed on others in either a market or a command economy? Why? (*It is virtually impossible to define property rights to some kinds of resources, such as air, rivers, and oceans; and many disputes over the use of these resources involve millions of people, thousands*

of firms, and sometimes several different national governments. Therefore, the conditions for the Coase theorem will rarely hold in these disputes in either market or command economies.*) Do you believe the Coase theorem would resolve more disputes involving economic damages imposed on others in market or command economies? Why? (*Although the Coase theorem cannot resolve many disputes over economic damages, because property rights are typically stronger in market economies, it is more likely to resolve more disputes in market economies than in command economies.*)

ASSESSMENT

1. Did the former Soviet Union feature more or less private ownership of resources than the United States? Do you believe the different pattern of ownership affected the efficiency of those economies?

2. (Optional) Assign students to research different countries and economic systems in terms of property rights, private and public ownership of property, economic performance (GDP, economic growth, standards of living), and environmental quality. Compare the findings and share with the class as a whole.

Visual 1
Keeping Them Down on the Collective Farm

RECORD OF HARVESTS AND WAGE PAYMENTS

Harvest Totals		Total Wage Payments
Yield of Nutras	Yield of Vitas	Bucko$

Round 1 – Incentive: 10 Bucko$ for 10 nutras (REQUIRED),

| ____ | ____ | |

Round 2 – Incentive: 10 Bucko$ for 10 nutras (REQUIRED)
then 1 extra Bucko for each additional nutra

| ____ | ____ | ____ |

Round 3 – Incentive: 10 Bucko$ for 10 nutras (REQUIRED)
then 1 extra Bucko for each additional nutra,
and two extra Bucko$ for each additional vita.

| ____ | ____ | ____ |

Discussion Question: Did farmers produce as much as they could in each round? Why or why not?

Visual 2
Property Rights, The Tragedy of the Commons, and the Coase Theorem in Market and Command Economies

Discussion Questions:

1. How are property rights typically defined and enforced in market and command economies?

2. Would you expect to see more examples of "the tragedy of the commons" in market or command economies? Why?

3. Would the Coase theorem resolve all cases of economic damages imposed on others in either a market or a command economy? Why?

4. Do you believe the Coase theorem would resolve more disputes involving economic damages imposed on others in market or command economies? Why?

Activity 1
Keeping Them Down on the Collective Farm

You are a peasant farmer whose only livelihood is working and living on a collective farm, which is owned the state.

- Each working period you must deliver 10 nutras (the crop grown on the farm) to the state. In return, you will receive 10 Bucko$, which is just enough money to let you buy enough food and clothing to survive.

- The farm manager strongly encourages workers to produce more than 10 nutras each working period. However, there is currently no extra pay for this work.

- During the working period, you will simulate producing crops by coloring the nutras (or in a later round, vitas) on your worksheet. If you were really working on the farm, producing these crops would require a lot of hard work, so you are not likely to work more unless you are paid to work.

= 1 nutra   = 1 vita

Round 1 – Incentive: 10 Bucko$ for 10 nutras (REQUIRED)

Yield = _____

Earnings = _____

Activity 1
(Continued)

Round 2 – Incentive: 10 Bucko$ for 10 nutras (REQUIRED),
plus 1 extra Bucko for each additional nutra produced.

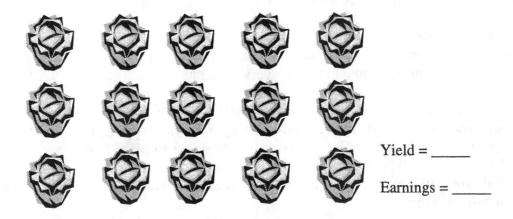

Yield = _____

Earnings = _____

Round 3 – Incentive: 10 Bucko$ for 10 nutras (REQUIRED),
plus 1 extra Bucko for each additional nutra produced,
and 2 extra Bucko$ for each vita produced.

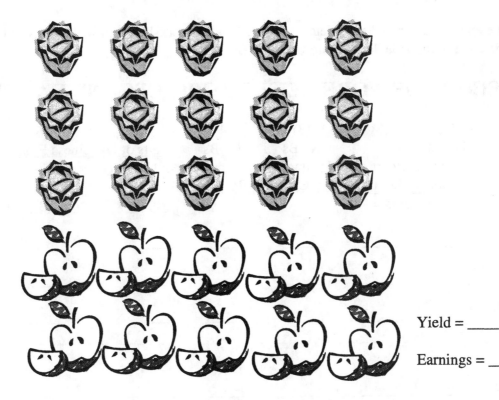

Yield = _____

Earnings = _____

Activity 2
Share and Share Alike

The society in which you live believes that all individuals have identical needs. Therefore, everyone receives an equal share of the total production in the economy. The only output produced in the economy is a product known as NUB.

Assume that your happiness as a consumer depends on two things: The number of NUBs you consume, and the amount of leisure time you have. In each round of the following activity, you will have 10 hours of time to devote to factory work or leisure.

Each hour you work, you can produce 1 NUB. All of the NUBs that you and others in your class produce will be divided equally. Every NUB you receive gives you 2 units of happiness. Every hour of leisure you take gives you 1 unit of happiness, but produces no NUBs. There will be four rounds in this activity. In each round, you will decide how to divide your 10 hours between leisure and work. Do what you think will result in the most units of happiness.

When each round begins, write down how many hours you will devote to work in column (1) and how many hours you will devote to leisure in column (2). These must add up to exactly 10. When all workers' choices have been added up and the total NUB production is determined, you will each receive an equal share of the NUBs.

At the end of each round, calculate and record on the worksheet below the units of happiness you receive in each round from leisure and from NUBs.

RECORD OF WORK/LEISURE CHOICES AND HAPPINESS

	(1) Hours You Work (Total Hours = 10)	(2) Hours of Leisure	(3) NUBs Produced by Class	(4) NUBs You Receive	(5) Units of Happiness From: NUBs col. (4) x 2	(6) Leisure col. (2) x 1	(7) Total Units of Happiness col. (5) + col. (6)
Round 1	____	____	____	____	____	____	____
Round 2	____	____	____	____	____	____	____
Round 3	____	____	____	____	____	____	____
Round 4	____	____	____	____	____	____	____

From *Focus: Economic Systems*, © National Council on Economic Education, New York, NY

Activity 3
Home in the Cupboard or Home on the Range: A Commons Tragedy

Part A – Home in the Cupboard

Consider the following "reconstructed" nursery rhyme:

Sweet Mother Hubbard went to her cupboard
To get her dear children some food
But when she got there it was tragically bare
Now they're all in a common bad mood.

Mrs. Hubbard has ten children, and the cupboard that holds the family food supply is open to everyone in the family. This is known as common ownership. Yesterday Mrs. Hubbard filled the cupboard with favorite treats for all to enjoy, including 20 cinnamon rolls. Based on the nursery rhyme, how did the children behave with these common ownership rules for food? Do you think each child ate two cinnamon rolls?

Suppose that next week Mrs. Hubbard once again fills the cupboard with treats, but announces a new family food rule. Each child will be assigned property rights to two cinnamon rolls. Anyone caught eating the rolls of others will be punished and receive no treats for several weeks. How are the children likely to behave under these rules?

Extension exercise:

Write short answers to the following questions, discuss them in small groups, then have one group member report your group's answers to the class.

Which is more likely to remain clean, a public restroom or a bathroom in your home or apartment? Why?

Which is more likely to be well maintained, the outside grounds or interior living areas of an apartment complex? Does it matter if the apartments are condominiums (owned by the people who live in them), or they are all owned by one private owner, or owned by the government? Why?

Activity 3 (continued)

Part B – Home on the Range

Round 1. You are one of ten residents of a small community interested in maximizing the individual return on your investment. Each of you has $100 to invest. Your investment choices are: buy a bond for $100 that is worth $110 (principal and interest) at the end of the investment period; or buy a brood of chickens that will be raised as "free range" birds and then sold for profit. If you invest in the birds, they will be free to roam on a common feeding ground and you will incur no extra costs for chicken feed or maintenance. At the end of the investment period, the bonds will be cashed and the brood will be sold by weight, to determine the return on your investment. The chicken brood weights are a function of how many other birds are also feeding on the common ground. The chickens will weigh less if there are more of them competing for food on the commons. A chart of expected brood weights is given below. The market price for these chickens is $1 per pound. Based on this information, how many residents will buy broods and how many will buy bonds? Explain your answer.

Number of Broods	Expected Average Weight of Each Brood	Total Weight of All Broods Combined
	(Pounds at end of investment period)	
0	0	0
1	120	120
2	116	232
3	111	333
4	105	420
5	100	500

Round 2. Now suppose the community elects one person to determine how to invest all of the money from the community in order to maximize the total investment income for the community. How many bonds and broods would be purchased?

Round 3. Suppose the common feeding area is sold to a single private owner who will raise chickens. How many broods of chickens will that person raise in each investment period?

Activity 4
The Coase Theorem

The conditions necessary for the Coase theorem to apply are:
- Property rights are well defined, and
- Negotiating costs are zero or small.

When both conditions are met, the Coase theorem predicts that in disputes about damages to someone else's property:
- The same efficient outcome is achieved regardless of who is assigned the property rights and who pays the damages.
- Government enforcement is not required to reach the efficient outcome.

To see how this works, consider the following example:

Mochabucks is a successful coffee shop located in a strip mall. The retail space next door was vacant until recently, when Megadent Auto Body Shop opened for business. There are no other vacant properties in the strip mall. Mochabucks earned $400 per day in profits before the Body Shop opened. But Megadents creates a lot of loud noise and smelly paint fumes. Many customers stopped coming to Mochabucks, and as a result its profits are now zero. The owner of Mochabucks is demanding that Megadent reduce the noise and fumes, but Megadent's owners refuse. They say the noise and fumes are an inevitable by-product of the dent-repair business, which brings in $1,000 per day in profits.

If laws in this city favor Mochabucks, so that Megadent is legally responsible for these damages to Mochabucks' profits, what could Megadent do to keep Mochabucks' owner happy? Would Megadent go out of business?

Now suppose the property rights to operate a business favor Megadent, and Mochabucks is not legally entitled to any damages from Megadent. What will happen in this case?

Activity 5 - Extension Exercise
Some Difficulties Applying the Coase Theorem

Using the Coase theorem to solve disputes involving air and water pollution is difficult because the necessary conditions are not met. Recall that in order for the Coase theorem to work, two conditions must apply:

- Property rights are well defined, and
- Negotiating costs are zero or small.

To understand why the Coase theorem doesn't lead to efficient outcomes in cases of air and water pollution, discuss the following questions:

Who owns the air and waterways?

How many people are affected by air and water pollution?

Would you expect air and water pollution to be worse in a command economy, where central authorities make economic decisions, or in a market economy with economic decisions made by thousands of buyers and sellers? Why?

 From *Focus: Economic Systems*, © National Council on Economic Education, New York, NY

LESSON FOUR
SPARTA, ATHENS, CUBA, AND THE UNITED STATES: ANCIENT AND MODERN EXAMPLES OF COMMAND AND MARKET ECONOMIES

INTRODUCTION

Command and market economies both have long histories, which continue even today, despite the recent dissolution of the former Soviet Union. This lesson first examines differences between the economic systems of ancient Sparta and Athens. Then it reviews similar kinds of differences between two contemporary economic systems – the United States and Cuba. The comparisons in both cases focus on political and economic freedoms provided under the different systems.

CONCEPTS

Economic institutions
Market economy
Command economy
Economic freedom
Property rights

CONTENT STANDARDS

There is an economic role for government to play in a market economy whenever the benefit of a government policy outweighs its costs. Governments often provide for national defense, address environmental concerns, define and protect property rights, and attempt to make markets more competitive. Most government policies also redistribute income.

Institutions evolve in market economies to help individuals and groups accomplish their goals. Banks, labor unions, corporations, legal systems, and not-for-profit organizations are examples of important institutions. A different kind of institution, clearly defined and enforced property rights, is also essential to a market economy.

BENCHMARKS

An important role for government in the economy is to define, establish, and enforce private property rights. A property right to a good or service includes the right to exclude others from using the good or service and the right to transfer the ownership or use of the resources to others.

Property rights, contract enforcement, standards for weights and measures, and liability rules affect incentives for people to produce and exchange goods and services.

OBJECTIVES

♦ Students identify the characteristics of market and command economies in ancient Athens and Sparta.

♦ Students identify the characteristics of market and command economies in the current economies of the United States and Cuba.

LESSON DESCRIPTION

Students compare the economies of ancient Sparta and Athens using primary sources of speeches and other historical accounts. Students then compare the current economic systems of the United States and Cuba, using passages from their respective national constitutions.

TIME REQUIRED

Two class periods.

MATERIALS

- Visual 1: Economic Freedom
- Visual 2: The Economy of Ancient Greece
- Visual 3: Economic Freedom in Ancient Athens and Sparta

- Visual 4: Private Ownership Provisions of the U.S. Constitution
- Visual 5: Government Ownership Provisions of the Cuban Constitution
- Activity 1: Comparing Economic Systems: Athens and Sparta
- Activity 2: Comparing Economic Systems: The United States and Cuba

If you would like your students to act the parts of Greek orators, consider obtaining Greek robes or costumes for the students to wear when they read the statements of Pericles and Lycurgus.

PROCEDURES

1. Explain that examples of market and command economies have existed for centuries, and even millennia. The first examples discussed in this lesson occurred in ancient Greece, during the time of a great rivalry between the city-states of Athens and Sparta. The second examples are the current economic systems also used by two neighboring countries – the United States and Cuba.

Note that every society has a system of laws that governs economic and political behavior. One basis for comparing economic systems is to analyze the amount of individual freedom permitted by the laws and institutions of a society. Begin a class discussion by asking students to list some examples of *political* freedoms that are provided under the U.S. Constitution. *(List the major freedoms provided under the Bill of Rights, including freedom of religion, speech, press, assembly and so forth.)*

2. Your students will probably not understand the idea of economic freedom as well as they understand political freedoms. Display Visual 1 and discuss these types of economic freedom, inviting students to suggest additional examples of restrictions on economic freedoms.

3. Explain that the appropriate degree of both political and economic freedoms have been debated and even fought over for thousands of years. Point out that a famous early example occurred in ancient Greece, and a contemporary example involves the United States and Cuba. Announce that the class will try to draw some parallels between these two cases. To provide a general overview of economic conditions in ancient Greece, display Visual 2 and briefly review the items listed there.

A. While the economy of ancient Greece was predominantly agricultural, with little large-scale industry and fairly primitive production technologies, it did have many of the basic characteristics of a market economy.

B. The period between 800 and 50 BC was a time of growing specialization, division of labor, and an increase in both internal and international trade. As trade increased, the currency-based sectors of the economy expanded. The economy depended heavily on slaves to produce many goods and services.

C. A system of individual ownership of land and other resources evolved.

D. A system of largely free trade – without tariffs, quotas, or other legal and economic barriers – was established for internal (domestic) trade.

E. The sea was perhaps the most important natural resource of the ancient Greeks, because shipping and trading by water was easier and less expensive than shipping by land. Eventually the Greeks launched trading operations that resulted in ports and cities being established along extensive parts of the coasts of the Mediterranean and the Black Seas.

F. Trading across larger areas, with more people and lands that offered a wider range of resources, increased the level of income throughout the empire. Greek colonies enjoyed unrestricted access to markets on mainland Greece and traded wheat, meat, dried fish, hides, wool, timber, and basic metals in exchange for mainland finished products such as pottery, perfumes, and works of art in addition to grapes, wine, and olives. Trade was not completely unfettered. For security reasons, government restrictions were maintained on grain imports to insure supplies to Greece. Grain supplies to the ancient Greeks – and later the Romans – were somewhat like oil supplies are to contemporary Western democracies and Japan.

G. The ancient Greeks developed coined money that made transactions easier, which increased specialization and trade even more. The first Greek coins were made of electrum, a natural alloy of silver and gold. The right to issue coins soon became a monopoly of the state. The imprint of kings or other rulers was stamped on coins to guarantee the value of the metal in the coins and to honor the rulers.

4. Explain that the leaders of ancient Greece were famous for their skills as public speakers, and that Pericles was a famous orator. Ask a student with good reading and speaking skills to read the excerpt from Pericles' Funeral Speech and the statement of economic historian Douglass North. Encourage the reader to act the part by standing in front of the room and putting on Greek robes or a "laurel" wreath during this short address.

5. Distribute Activity 1 to the class. Have students read Part 1, and then ask: Who was Pericles? *(Pericles led ancient Athens during it most prosperous period [443-429 BC]. He helped establish the constitutional reforms that brought about full Athenian democracy. He opposed the economic system developed by Sparta.)* What were his ideas regarding economic freedom? *(He believed in property rights, and a free domestic trading market.)* What modern political leader seems most like Pericles? *(Answers will vary.)* Why do you agree or disagree with the ideas Pericles supported? *(Agree; property rights gave citizens incentives to work, because they could keep what they earned, or trade for what they wanted. Disagree; slavery persisted so all did not enjoy economic freedom.)*

6. Display Visual 3. Ask the class to explain how they would characterize economic freedoms under the system described by Pericles. Record their suggestions on Visual 3. A completed chart is shown on the next page, following procedure 12.

7. Ask another student with good reading and speaking skills to read the excerpt on Lycurgus from Plutarch's *Lives of the Noble Greeks and Romans*. Again, encourage the reader to act the part by standing in front of the room and putting on Greek robes, a laurel wreath, or perhaps a soldiers' costume during this short address.

8. Direct students' attention back to Activity 1. Have students read the first paragraph in Part 2, then ask: Who was Lycurgus? *(Lycurgus is regarded as the creator of the ideals of strict military discipline and asceticism in Sparta. He is credited with having saved Sparta from a slave rebellion.)* What were his ideas regarding economic freedom? *(Lycurgas believed wealth was the cause of most problems, so he ended property rights and discouraged trade by changing from coins with value to worthless coins.)* What modern political leader seems most like Lycurgus? *(Answers will vary.)* Did Plutarch seem to agree or disagree with the ideas Lycurgus supported? Do you agree or disagree with them? *(Plutarch seems to agree that Lycurgus addressed real*

problems. Plutarch had no sympathy for the rich.)

9. Display Visual 3 again. Ask the class to explain how they would characterize economic freedoms under the system described by Lycurgus. Record their suggestions on Visual 3. A completed chart appears below.

10. Explain that some contemporary economic systems are nearly as different from one another as those of ancient Athens and Sparta. A good example of this is a comparison of the economic systems of the United States and Cuba. One way to show these differences is by comparing parts of the national constitutions for these two countries.

11. Distribute Activity 2. Have students read Part 1, then display Visual 4. Ask students to describe how these provisions of the U.S. Constitution protect private property rights and economic freedom. Record their suggestions on Visual 4. A completed chart appears on the next page.

12. Have students read Part 2 of Activity 2, then display Visual 5. Ask students to describe how these provisions of the Cuban Constitution establish government ownership rights. Record their suggestions on Visual 5. A completed chart appears on the next page.

Visual 3 (Completed)
Economic Freedom in Ancient Athens and Sparta

Economic Freedom	Athens	Sparta
Freedom for individuals to own and use property as they choose	*People were free to own land, and to buy and sell land.*	*The state determined the pattern of land ownership.*
Freedom to make voluntary exchanges between individuals, regions, and nations	*Internal trade was free. External grain trade was permitted under some state controls.*	*The use of money—silver and gold—was restricted to limit or even end trading.*
Freedom for individuals to use their income as they wish	*People could buy or sell the goods and services they chose, and consume what they purchased.*	*People had little choice regarding the food they ate.*

Visual 4 (Completed)
Private Ownership Provisions of the U.S. Constitution

Location in the Constitution	Provisions for Private Property Rights
Article I, Section 10	*People can enter into legal contracts with other individuals or firms. These contracts are legally binding and cannot be voided by actions of state or local governments.*
Amendment V	*It is illegal for anyone, including the government, to seize a person or a person's property. Exceptions are allowed, but only following legal procedures, in cases where a person's property or money is taken to repay contractual debts, or when the government claims the right of eminent domain to seize property, but must provide fair compensation following due process.*
Amendment XIV	*Explicitly states that the provisions of Amendment V, above, also apply to state and local governments.*
Amendment X	*Final powers—including basic political and economic freedoms—are held by state and local representatives, and by the people themselves. Decentralized power and decision-making is recognized as the rule, not an exception.*

Visual 5 (Completed)
Government Ownership Provisions of the Cuban Constitution

Location in the Constitution	Provision for Government Ownership Rights
Article 5	*The Communist Party is to lead society in the construction of a socialist and eventually communist economy and political state.*
Article 14	*The government, not individuals, owns the means of production.*
Article 15	*The government, not individuals, owns the land and all enterprises.*
Article 16	*The government, not individuals, makes basic economic decisions.*

CLOSURE

Conclude the lesson by asking students to compare ancient Athens and Sparta, and the United States and Cuba. Specifically, ask students:

1. In what ways are the economic systems of the United States and ancient Athens similar? *(Both favor private ownership and extensive economic freedom for individuals, and privately owned businesses.)*

2. In what ways are the economic systems of the United States and ancient Athens different? *(The economic freedoms of ancient Athens only extended to free citizens. Slavery in Athens—as in many parts of the ancient world – was widespread. There is less emphasis on government controls of grain markets in the United States, although the government does provide some subsidies to farmers and helps find export markets for some grains and other agricultural products.)*

3. In what ways are the economic systems of Cuba and ancient Sparta similar? *(Both feature a strong state role in economic decisions, and sharply limited economic*

freedom for individuals and privately owned businesses.)

4.   In what ways are the economic systems of Cuba and ancient Sparta different? *(Conditions in ancient Sparta may have been even more severe than they are in Cuba. Sparta, like Athens, depended heavily on slavery to maintain its standard of living. The greatest difference was Sparta's measures to eliminate money and limit trade, production, and consumption. In effect, Sparta adopted central planning to promote a self-sufficient, austere life, while Cuba hoped to achieve higher levels of production and consumption under a socialist state.)*

ASSESSMENT

Suppose there are two most excellent time travelers, Bill and Ted, who visit ancient Athens and Sparta, and then jump forward to modern Cuba and the United States. In two paragraphs, note the major similarities and differences Bill and Ted notice between these political and economic systems, and in the standards of living in the four economies, including the range of goods and services that people consume.

    From *Focus: Economic Systems*, © National Council on Economic Education, New York, NY

Visual 1
Economic Freedom

Economic Freedoms	Examples of Freedoms	Examples of Restrictions on Economic Freedoms
Freedom for individuals to own and use property as they choose	Buy a house, farm, or business of your choice	Required to pay property taxes and taxes on earnings or profits to pay for government services
Freedom to make voluntary exchanges between individuals, regions, and nations	Owners of clothing stores may purchase clothing made in other nations and offer them for sale	The government sometimes taxes or limits imports of certain products
Freedom for individuals to use their income as they wish	Buy a car of your choice	Required to obey traffic laws and have a license to drive

Visual 2
The Economy of Ancient Greece

- The Greek city-states developed a system of individual land ownership and the right to buy or sell products made in these areas.

- Easy access to the sea permitted trade to flourish.

- The Greek colonies had unrestricted access to markets on the Greek mainland. The colonies traded wheat, meat, dried fish, hides, wool, timber, and basic metals.

- People on the Greek mainland produced finished products to trade, such as wine, pottery, perfumes, and works of art.

- The Greeks used coined money to make trading easier, leading to a greater expansion of trade.

From *Focus: Economic Systems,* © National Council on Economic Education, New York, NY

Visual 3
Economic Freedom in Ancient Athens and Sparta

Economic Freedom	Athens	Sparta
Freedom for individuals to own and use property as they choose		
Freedom to make voluntary exchanges between individuals, regions, and nations		
Freedom for individuals to use their income as they wish		

Visual 4
Private Ownership Provisions of the U.S. Constitution

Location in the Constitution	Provisions for Private Property Rights
Article I, Section 10	
Amendment V	
Amendment XIV	
Amendment X	

From *Focus: Economic Systems*, © National Council on Economic Education, New York, NY

Visual 5
Government Ownership Provisions of the Cuban Constitution

Location in the Constitution	Provisions for Government Ownership
Article 5	
Article 14	
Article 15	
Article 16	

Activity 1
Comparing Economic Systems: Athens and Sparta

Part 1: Pericles and the Golden Age of Athens

Although the economic systems of many of the Greek city-states were similar, there were some important differences. Perhaps the greatest differences were between the city-states of Athens and Sparta. One way to think about the differences is to see Athens—under the influence of Pericles – as having many of the characteristics of a democratic market economy. Sparta – under the laws of Lycurgus – had many characteristics of a command economy and political system.

Pericles (495-429 BC) helped gain approval of the constitutional reforms that brought about the full Athenian democracy in 461 BC. He presided over the Golden Age and most prosperous period for ancient Athens (443-429 BC). A general and statesman, Pericles became virtually an uncrowned king. He had a public reputation for honesty, but politically he was regarded as a radical. He was a staunch opponent of Sparta. His hostility toward Sparta brought about the Peloponnesian War (431-404 BC).

Renowned for his oratory, his famous Funeral Speech (431 or 430 BC), as recorded by Thucydides, describes some of his ideas about Athens' democratic principles:

Our constitution is called a democracy because power is in the hands not of a minority but of the whole people. When it is a question of settling private disputes, everyone is equal before the law, when it is a question of putting one person before another in positions of public responsibility, what counts is not membership of a particular class, but the actual ability which the man possesses.... And, just as our political life is free and open, so is our day-to-day life in our relations with each other. We do not get into a state with our next door neighbor if he enjoys himself in his own way. We are free and tolerant in our private lives; but in public affairs we keep to the law.

The Nobel-laureate economic historian Douglass North wrote the following about the economy of Athens during the time of Pericles:

In this case a free internal market for goods and services on the one hand provided ownership rights ...in land, capital, and labor and, on the other, controlled international trade in grain to guarantee a food supply.

Questions for Discussion:

Who was Pericles?

What were his ideas regarding economic freedom?

What modern political leader seems most like Pericles?

Why do you agree or disagree with the ideas Pericles supported?

Activity 1 (continued)

Part 2 Lycurgus and the Military State of Sparta

Lycurgus is the legendary lawgiver of Sparta. He is credited with making the Spartan ideals of harsh military discipline a model for the entire Spartan economy. There is some disagreement among historians about whether or not there really was such a person, but some scholars claim his measures were instrumental in preventing a second helot (slave) revolt.

The Roman historian Plutarch wrote the following description of Lycurgus' policies:

Lycurgus addressed the question of land ownership. At this time, there was extreme inequality among the Spartans, with most of the wealth and land in the control of only a few. Most of the people felt poor and unhappy. Arrogance and envy, luxury and crime, resulted from this unequal distribution of property. Lycurgus divided the land equally. So that merit – not money – became the only measure of a man's worth.

Lycurgus intended to remove any inequalities in ownership of personal property as well as real property. ...His solution was to ban ownership of gold or silver, and to allow only money made of iron. Iron coins of Sparta were dipped in vinegar to make the metal brittle and worthless. Merchants laughed at this money because it had no intrinsic value, so imports of luxuries stopped.

The most effective measure against the love of money was Lycurgus' law that all meals had to be eaten together in public mess halls. Everyone ate the same thing, so money could not buy dainty food. And since the rich could not eat at home, there was no way for them to show off their fancy things. The rich could no longer spend their lives at home, lying on their couches and stuffing themselves with unwholesome delicacies, like pigs being fattened for slaughter.

Questions for Discussion:

Who was Lycurgus?

What were his ideas regarding economic freedom?

What modern political leader seems most like Lycurgus?

Did Plutarch seem to agree or disagree with the ideas Lycurgus supported? Do you agree or disagree with them?

Activity 2
Comparing Economic Systems: The United States and Cuba

Property Rights in a Market Economy
Markets are places where goods and services are traded, and people can trade things that they own. Therefore, in this respect the most basic economic freedom is the right to own and use property as you wish. This freedom, like all others, has some restrictions – for example, it is illegal to buy or sell some products. Nevertheless, clearly defined property rights that are effectively enforced by a nation's legal system are a fundamental characteristic of a market economy.

Read each of the quotations below, taken from the Constitution of the United States. Be prepared to discuss how these provisions protect the right to own, buy, and sell private property.

Part 1 Excerpts from the United States Constitution
Article I, Section 10.
"No State shall…coin Money; emit Bills of Credit; make any Thing but gold and silver Coin a Tender in Payment of Debts; pass any Bill of Attainder, ex post facto Law, or Law impairing the Obligations of Contracts…."

Amendment V
"No person shall…be deprived of life, liberty, or property, without due process of law…."

Amendment XIV. Section 1.
"No State shall…deprive any person of life, liberty, or property, without due process of law; …nor deny to any person within its jurisdiction the equal protection of the laws."

Amendment X
"The powers not delegated to the United States by the Constitution, nor prohibited by it to the States, are reserved to the States respectively, or to the people."

Property Rights in a Command Economy
The most basic characteristic of a command economy is central planning to determine the allocation of resources, rather than allowing individuals and privately-owned firms to decide how to use the resources. In communist and socialist economies, factories, heavy machinery, and in many cases other kinds of businesses and resources are owned by the state. That makes it very clear who will decide how those resources will be used.

Read each of the quotations below from the Constitution of the Republic of Cuba (revised in 1992). Be prepared to discuss how these provisions strengthen the state's right to own property, and limit property rights for individuals and privately-owned firms.

Activity 2 (continued)

Part 2 Excerpts from the Constitution of the Republic of Cuba

Article 5
"The Communist Party of Cuba…is the superior leading force of the society and the state, that organizes and orients the common efforts toward the lofty ends of the construction of socialism and the advance toward the communist society."

Article 14
"In the Cuban Republic the economic system is based on the socialistic ownership of all the fundamental means of production…."

"Also, the principle of socialist distribution of each according to his capacity, and to each according to his labor, governs."

Article 15
"These are socialist state properties of all the people:
    a) Land that does not pertain to the small farmers or cooperatives…
    b) Sugar refineries, factories, fundamental (basic) means of transportation, and whatever enterprises, banks and installations have been nationalized and expropriated from the imperialists, estate owners and the bourgeois, as well as the factories, economic enterprises and installations and scientific, social and cultural centers and sports buildings…"

Article 16
"The state organizes, directs and controls the economic national activity according to a plan that guarantees the proper development of the country to the end of strengthening the socialist system…."

LESSON FIVE
ANYTHING PLANNERS DO, MARKETS DO . . . .

INTRODUCTION

The basic economic questions facing any economic system are deciding *what* goods to produce, *how* to produce them, and *who* will consume them. In any economic system resources can be used to produce some, but not all, of the things people want. But market and command economies use very different ways to decide what products are produced, as well as how and for whom. Determining how to produce a good or service involves deciding – from innumerable alternatives – which resources to use, in what combinations, and with what technology. Once the production takes place, there must also be some process that determines how those resources will be distributed, recognizing that for most goods and services when one person or firm consumes a product it is used up, and therefore not available for other people or firms to use.

In market economies, these decisions are guided by the relative prices of goods, services, and productive resources. These prices are determined by the forces of supply and demand. Supply reflects the cost of producing or providing a good or service compared to the price producers think consumers will pay. Demand is based on choices made by individual consumers, who decide how many units of a product they are willing and able to buy at different prices. In command economies key supply decisions are made by central planners who attempt to achieve certain social goals, typically without reference to market prices. In this lesson students experience some of those different procedures, and then discuss which procedures they believe are most efficient and equitable.

CONCEPTS
Scarcity
Market economy
Command economy
Resource allocation
Technology

CONTENT STANDARDS

Different methods can be used to allocate goods and services. People, acting individually or collectively through government, must choose which methods to use to allocate different kinds of goods and services.

Markets exist when buyers and sellers interact. This interaction determines market prices and thereby allocates scarce goods and services.

BENCHMARKS

There are essential differences between a market economy, in which allocations result from individuals making decisions as buyers and sellers, and a command economy, in which resources are allocated according to central authority.

Market prices are determined through the buying and selling decisions made by buyers and sellers.

Relative price refers to the price of one good or service compared to the prices of other goods and services. Relative prices are the basic measures of the relative scarcity of products when prices are set by market forces (supply and demand).

OBJECTIVES

◆   Students explain why scarcity requires people to choose how to allocate resources in any kind of economic system.

◆   Students compare and contrast market and command economies.

♦ Students describe the role that prices play in resource allocation in market and command economies.

♦ Students identify the least-cost method of production.

LESSON DESCRIPTION

Students assume roles as decision-makers and allocate resources in the framework of both a command and market economy. In the first round, students role-play members of GrossComm, a central planning committee responsible for determining what (how many) goods will be produced and how resources will be combined to produce them. In the second round, students role-play resource owners and producers of goods in a market economy, making decisions about what (how many) to produce and identifying the least-cost method of production.

TIME REQUIRED

One to two class periods.

MATERIALS

- Visual 1: Plato and Ropa Production Techniques
- Visual 2: Plato and Ropa Production Techniques and Resources Prices
- Visual 3: The Demand for Obreros
- Visual 4: Market and Command Economies
- Activity 1: GrossComm Decision-Making Cards, two copies cut apart
- Activity 2: Obrero Cards, two copies cut apart
- Activity 3: Plato and Ropa Producer Cards, one copy cut apart
- Activity 4: Dineros, five copies cut apart

PROCEDURES

1. Discuss or review the following ideas. The fundamental economic problem of scarcity — the idea that human wants for goods and services exceed what can be produced with available resources — requires an economic system to answer three basic questions: 1) what goods and services will be produced, 2) how they will be produced, and 3) who will consume them. Every economic system must have procedures to decide how to allocate scarce resources in answering these three basic questions.

2. Explain that students will participate in two rounds of an activity to see how resources are allocated in two countries — Estado and Mercado. For simplicity in the activity, only two goods are produced in both economies — platos (food) and ropas (clothing). Both platos and ropas are made using three kinds of productive resources – terras (land or natural resources), obreros (labor or human resources), and maquinas (capital resources).

3. Display Visual 1, and explain that the top table shows alternative methods for producing platos. The bottom table shows alternative methods for producing ropas. Make sure students understand that one megaunit of platos can be produced using technology A with 8 units of terras, 2 units of obreros, and 4 units of maquinas; **or** using technology B with 4 units of terras, 6 units of obreros, and 2 units of maquinas; **or** using technology C with 2 units of terras, 8 units of obreros, and 4 units of maquinas. One megaunit of ropas can be produced using technology X with 2 units of terras, 4 units of obreros, and 6 units of maquinas; **or** using technologies Y or Z and the units of resources shown in Visual 1.

4. Announce that, in the first round of the activity, students will see how platos and ropas are produced in the country of Estado. Divide the class into six groups of 3-5 students, giving each group a card from Activity 1. These three cards are identical except for the "Note" at the bottom of the card. Have two groups work independently with each of the three different "Notes." Have one member of each group read the card aloud to the others. Explain that each group must select a production technology and decide how many platos and ropas to produce,

given the information on its card and on Visual 1. One group member should serve as a reporter. Give the groups 5 to 10 minutes to make their two decisions – which production technique to use and how many platos and ropas to produce.

5. Have each group reporter tell which production technology his or her group chose, and how many platos and ropas the group decided to produce. Check to be sure that the amount of production reported could be carried out using the available units of productive resources. Have each reporter explain why the group made the decisions it made. Explore in a class discussion why resource allocations differed among the groups.

(The decisions were based on what goals the planners thought to be most important based partly or entirely on the Notes on their cards. For example, some may have used production techniques requiring a lot of obreros because they were trying to maximize employment. It is possible, however, that even the groups working with the same Notes on their cards made different decisions, based on the goals of the individuals in the groups, or differences in calculations concerning the best technologies to use in producing platos and ropas. Emphasize the idea that different planners make different decisions, based on the goals they want to pursue and their ideas about the most efficient way to produce outputs.

You may want to mention that in the former Soviet Union, planners chose to devote a lot of resources to producing capital goods (factories and machines) and military goods, which meant there was less production of consumer goods.

If questions about the price or value of platos, ropas, or productive resources are raised during the discussion, explain that in a centrally planned economy those prices would be assigned by the planners, too. Therefore, those prices would also reflect the planners' ideas about what things are most important, or

the best way to distribute goods and productive resources in the economy. That is very different from the way prices are determined in a market economy, as they will see in round 2 of the activity. If students made decisions that equated a megaunit of platos with a megaunit of ropas, or the value of units of the different productive inputs, that is something that they – not consumers – assumed or decided for their economy.)

6. Announce that in round 2 students will see how resources are allocated in the country of Mercado, which has a market economy. Explain that they will play a role as business managers in competing companies that produce either platos or ropas, or as workers who will be hired to work for one of these companies. The business managers want to maximize profits. Workers prefer higher wages to lower wages, assuming that other job benefits and working conditions are equivalent. Before assigning roles, display Visual 2 and explain that although the production technologies for platos and ropas have not changed from those used in round 1, the business managers can now purchase as much terras and maquinas as they want in the marketplace, at the prices shown. Note that here a unit of maquinas is 50 percent more expensive (15 dineros) than a unit of terras (10 dineros). Discuss the following:

A. Will the price information for maquinas and terras be helpful to the business managers? (*Yes, it will help them calculate production costs and determine the most efficient technology to use.*)

B. Why would a producer be interested in the cost of production? (*Businesses will maximize profits only by using the least-cost method of production.*)

C. Will business managers require more information to determine the least-cost technology? (*Yes, the price of obreros is unknown.*)

7. Announce that students will now participate in an activity on labor markets to determine the price of obreros in Mercado. Divide the class into three groups of about eight students each. Give each student in the first group an Obrero Owner card, give each student in the second group a Plato Producer card, and each student in the third group a Ropa Producer card. Give each student in the two producer groups the number of dineros indicated in the top right corner of the card he or she receives. (Important: This is six times the price on each card, because each producer wants to buy six units of obreros from 8 workers.) If you have fewer than 24 students participating, eliminate an equal number of plato and ropa producers, starting with the cards that show the lowest values for a unit of obreros. If you have more than 24 students participating, add an equal number of plato and ropa producers, again beginning with cards that show the lowest values for a unit of obreros.

8. Explain that obrero owners and plato and ropa producers form a market to exchange units of obreros (which are units or work/effort, such as hours of work) for dineros. Tell students that they should follow the instructions on their cards very carefully, and **make sure that all students understand that workers will sell all six of their units of obreros to one firm, for one price that the buyers and sellers will negotiate. Similarly, the firm managers will buy all six units of obreros from one seller, at one price.** Stress that obrero owners are trying to get the highest possible price, and plato and ropa producers are trying to purchase obreros at the lowest possible price. It will probably pay buyers and sellers to shop around and look for the best deal they can find. **Tell the buyers and sellers to write down the names of students with whom they trade, and the price for one unit of obreros at which they agree to trade.** Designate an area in the classroom for trading. Once students understand their roles and assignments, allow 5-10 minutes for exchanges. Near the end of the trading session, warn

students when there are about two minutes remaining.

9. Ask the plato producers how many units of obreros they purchased, then ask the ropa producers the same question. *(Given the values on the producer cards, all of the units of obreros should have been purchased. If there were eight obrero sellers, 36 units [from six obrero sellers] should be purchased by plato producers and 12 units [from two obrero sellers] by ropa producers. To show students why that is true, display Visual 3, which shows the demand for obreros from both plato and ropa producers. If there were eight obrero sellers, a total of 48 units should be sold. Point out that all 48 units would be purchased at a price of 12 dineros. If there were not eight obrero sellers, identify what price would clear the market for the number of units that were available in your class.)* Ask all of the producers to report the prices they paid for obreros. *(Students may report different prices, especially for exchanges that took place early in the trading round. If you had eight obrero sellers offering 48 units of obreros, most trades should take place at a price of 12 dineros, as shown in Visual 3. If you do not get this result in the classroom simulation, explain that a price of 12 dineros would have evolved if everyone had more information and more time to trade. [Or a higher/lower price if you used more/fewer obrero sellers in you class.])*

10. Write 12d in the blank spaces for obreros on Visual 2, on the tables for producing platos and ropas. Then have all students work in pairs, using the price information for all three productive resources, to determine which production technologies will minimize production costs in making platos and ropas. Remind students that producers want to minimize costs to maximize profits. *(If you had more/fewer obrero sellers, and therefore higher/lower price for obreros, you may still want to use a price of 12d in this and the following steps, by asking students to determine*

From *Focus: Economic Systems,* © National Council on Economic Education, New York, NY

what price would have prevailed with eight obrero sellers. Otherwise you will have to recalculate some numbers as you work through the rest of the activity.)

11. Have some pairs report which technology they selected to produce a megaunit of platos and explain why they chose it. *(Technology B is the least-cost method of production for one megaunit of platos, 142d = 40d for terras + 72d for obreros + 30d for maquinas. Technology A costs 164d; technology C costs 176d.)*

12. Have other pairs report which technology they selected to produce a megaunit of ropas and explain why they chose it. *(Technology Z is the least-cost method of production for one megaunit of ropas, 133d = 40d for terras + 48d for obreros + 45d for maquinas. Technology X costs 158d; technology Y costs 186d.)*

13. Ask students to compare the technologies they chose when acting as central planners in Estado to the technologies they chose in Mercado, when market prices for productive resources were known. Consider each of the following topics.

   A. Why didn't all of the central-planning groups choose the same production technologies and the same amount of platos and ropas to produce? *(The decisions of the planners depended on what they believed were the most important goals to achieve, and on what they felt were the most effective production technologies without having input prices to use in making that decision. Not all groups had the same goals or viewed everything the same.)*

   B. Why did most or all students come to the same conclusions about production technology in the market economy? *(Decisions were based on finding the least-cost production technology, and in*

this activity all firms had access to the same technology and market prices for inputs/productive resources. You may want to note that sometimes different companies in market economies use different technologies because they operate larger or smaller facilities, or facilities that are relatively older or newer, or because they have invented and perhaps even patented new technologies.)

   C. How was the price of obreros determined? *(Through bargaining between businesses managers and obrero owners.)*

   D. What kept the price of obreros from being higher? *(Competition among the obreros owners.)*

   E. What kept the price of obreros from being lower? *(Competition among the plato and ropa producers.)*

   F. In Mercado, how would the prices for platos and ropas be determined? *(In market negotiations where the plato and ropa producers would act as sellers, and households would act as buyers. A market clearing price would evolve, with competition between sellers keeping prices from rising higher, while competition between buyers would keep prices from falling lower.)*

14. Explain that markets for productive resources (i.e., labor, natural resources, and capital) are directly linked to what can be produced with these resources, and to what consumers are willing and able to pay for the products. For example, in the Mercado activity the prices that producers were willing and able to pay for obreros reflected how much consumers were willing and able to pay for platos and ropas. Consumer demand for platos was high, and as a result more obreros were purchased by plato producers. This is the basic

way that market economies determine what to produce – reflecting the decisions made by individual consumers and producers in the marketplace.

15. Point out again that in market economies the basic economic question of how to produce (using different technologies and inputs) is also determined based on market prices reflecting individual decisions of buyers and sellers, as shown in the market activity. Producers consider the relative prices of resources to determine the least-cost method of production. Central planners may not have this kind of price information to work with, or they may decide to pursue objectives that they consider more important than efficient production or maximizing levels of production and consumption.

CLOSURE

Display Visual 4, and discuss the following.

1. In which country were resources owned and controlled by individuals? *(There was more decentralization and private ownership in Mercado; more collective ownership and central planning in Estado.)*

2. In Mercado, who decided what to produce? *(The decisions were based on the market values of platos and ropas and on the relative prices of the three resources — terras, obreros, and maquinas.)*

3. In Mercado, how were individuals motivated by self-interest? *(Obrero owners wanted higher prices to earn more income. Plato and ropa producers tried to pay lower prices to keep production costs low and profits high. The producers also sought the least-cost method of production to maximize profits.)*

4. In Estado, who decided how many platos and ropas would be produced and with what technology? *(Central planners, following whatever goals they felt were most important.)*

5. Based on the activities in this lesson, in your opinion under which of the economic systems used in these two countries would there be:

A. greater efficiency in production?

B. higher levels of consumption?

C. more economic freedom?

D. more unemployment?

E. higher prices?

F. greater equality of income?

G. more fairness in determining incomes?

(Market economies generally get high marks in the areas of freedom, efficiency, and achieving high levels of production/ consumption. Centrally planned economies may choose to emphasize other goals, perhaps including employment and income equality. Which system is fairer depends on personal views of how important these different goals and outcomes are. See Lesson 1, on economic goals in different kinds of economic systems.)

ASSESSMENT

Productive efficiency means producing goods and services at the lowest possible cost, without wasting productive resources such as labor, natural resources, and capital resources. Allocative efficiency means producing the things that satisfy as many of the most important wants in a society as possible. What major advantages and disadvantages do market economies and command economies have in trying to achieve productive efficiency and allocative efficiency?

Visual 1
Plato and Ropa Production Technologies

Resource	Technologies to Produce 1 Megaunit of Platos		
	A	B	C
Terras	8	4	2
Obreros	2	6	8
Maquinas	4	2	4

Resource	Technologies to Produce 1 Megaunit of Ropas		
	X	Y	Z
Terras	2	6	4
Obreros	4	8	4
Maquinas	6	2	3

Visual 2
Plato and Ropa Production Technologies and Resource Prices

Resource	Technologies to Produce 1 Megaunit of Platos			
	A	B	C	Price
Terras	8	4	2	10d
Obreros	2	6	8	__d
Maquinas	4	2	4	15d

Resource	Technologies to Produce 1 Megaunit of Ropas			
	X	Y	Z	Price
Terras	2	6	4	10d
Obreros	4	8	4	__d
Maquinas	6	2	3	15d

From *Focus: Economic Systems*, © National Council on Economic Education, New York, NY

Visual 3
The Demand for Obreros

Units of Obreros demanded by Plato and Ropa Producers at different prices

Price (dineros)	Units purchased by		
	Plato Producers	+ Ropa Producers	= Total
22	6	0	6
20	12	0	12
18	18	0	18
16	24	6	30
14	30	6	36
12	36	12	48
10	42	12	54
8	48	18	66
6	48	24	72
5	48	30	78
4	48	36	84
3	48	42	90
2	48	48	96

Visual 4
Market and Command Economies

MARKET ECONOMY

1. Productive resources are owned and controlled by individuals in the economy.

2. Decisions about how most resources are to be used are made by individual buyers and sellers in markets.

3. Individuals are motivated by their own self-interest.

COMMAND ECONOMY

1. Except for human resources, most productive resources are owned and controlled by the state or government.

2. Most decisions about how resources are to be used are made by central planners.

3. Central planners are motivated by social goals that they choose, or that are determined by political leaders.

From *Focus: Economic Systems*, © National Council on Economic Education, New York, NY

Activity 1
GrossComm Decision-Making Cards

You are a member of GrossComm, the central planning group of Estado. Your country produces two goods: platos (food) and ropas (clothing). Three resources are required to produce platos and ropas: terras (land), obreros (labor), and maquinas (capital). Estado has 48 units of each resource available to use this year. You must decide how to allocate these resources between platos and ropas; that is, how many platos and ropas you will produce. You must also choose a production technology that will determine the mix of inputs used to produce platos and ropas, given the production information on Visual 1. Be prepared to explain how you made your decisions.

Note: Estado's leaders want workers to have job security; that is, they want to be sure that all obreros are employed.

You are a member of GrossComm, the central planning group of Estado. Your country produces two goods: platos (food) and ropas (clothing). Three resources are required to produce platos and ropas: terras (land), obreros (labor), and maquinas (capital). Estado has 48 units of each resource available to use this year. You must decide how to allocate these resources between platos and ropas; that is, how many platos and ropas you will produce. You must also choose a production technology that will determine the mix of inputs used to produce platos and ropas, given the production information on Visual 1. Be prepared to explain how you made your decisions.

Note: Estado's leaders are very interested in maximizing the production of food and clothing, using the country's productive resources as efficiently as possible.

You are a member of GrossComm, the central planning group of Estado. Your country produces two goods: platos (food) and ropas (clothing). Three resources are required to produce platos and ropas: terras (land), obreros (labor), and maquinas (capital). Estado has 48 units of each resource available to use this year. You must decide how to allocate these resources between platos and ropas; that is, how many platos and ropas you will produce. You must also choose a production technology that will determine the mix of inputs used to produce platos and ropas, given the production information on Visual 1. Be prepared to explain how you made your decisions.

Note: Estado's leaders want the planning group to make consumers (who are also voters) in the country happy with the amounts of platos and ropas that are produced.

Activity 2
Obrero Cards

Obrero Owner

You own six units of obreros. Obreros is a labor resource used to produce platos (food) and ropas (clothes). You must sell all six units to one buyer, at one price, so try to sell them to the highest bidder. The higher the price you receive, the more income you will have to buy platos and ropas.

Obrero Owner

You own six units of obreros. Obreros is a labor resource used to produce platos (food) and ropas (clothes). You must sell all six units to one buyer, at one price, so try to sell them to the highest bidder. The higher the price you receive, the more income you will have to buy platos and ropas.

Obrero Owner

You own six units of obreros. Obreros is a labor resource used to produce platos (food) and ropas (clothes). You must sell all six units to one buyer, at one price, so try to sell them to the highest bidder. The higher the price you receive, the more income you will have to buy platos and ropas.

Obrero Owner

You own six units of obreros. Obreros is a labor resource used to produce platos (food) and ropas (clothes). You must sell all six units to one buyer, at one price, so try to sell them to the highest bidder. The higher the price you receive, the more income you will have to buy platos and ropas.

 From *Focus: Economic Systems*, © National Council on Economic Education, New York, NY

Activity 3
Plato and Ropa Producer Cards

Plato Producer	**Ropa Producer**
You are a producer of platos. You want to buy six units of obreros. Considering the demand for your product, the maximum you are willing and able to pay for one obreros unit is 22 dineros, but you want to pay a lower price if you can. Make a deal with an obrero owner.	You are a producer of ropas. You want to buy six units of obreros. Considering the demand for your product, the maximum you are willing and able to pay for one obreros unit is 16 dineros, but you want to pay a lower price if you can. Make a deal with an obrero owner.
Plato Producer	**Ropa Producer**
You are a producer of platos. You want to buy six units of obreros. Considering the demand for your product, the maximum you are willing and able to pay for one obreros unit is 20 dineros, but you want to pay a lower price if you can. Make a deal with an obrero owner.	You are a producer of ropas. You want to buy six units of obreros. Considering the demand for your product, the maximum you are willing and able to pay for one obreros unit is 12 dineros, but you want to pay a lower price if you can. Make a deal with an obrero owner.
Plato Producer	**Ropa Producer**
You are a producer of platos. You want to buy six units of obreros. Considering the demand for your product, the maximum you are willing and able to pay for one obreros unit is 18 dineros, but you want to pay a lower price if you can. Make a deal with an obrero owner.	You are a producer of ropas. You want to buy six units of obreros. Considering the demand for your product, the maximum you are willing and able to pay for one obreros unit is 8 dineros, but you want to pay a lower price if you can. Make a deal with an obrero owner.
Plato Producer	**Ropa Producer**
You are a producer of platos. You want to buy six units of obreros. Considering the demand for your product, the maximum you are willing and able to pay for one obreros unit is 16 dineros, but you want to pay a lower price if you can. Make a deal with an obrero owner.	You are a producer of ropas. You want to buy six units of obreros. Considering the demand for your product, the maximum you are willing and able to pay for one obreros unit is 6 dineros, but you want to pay a lower price if you can. Make a deal with an obrero owner.

Activity 3 (continued)

Plato Producer	**Ropa Producer**
You are a producer of platos. You want to buy six units of obreros. Considering the demand for your product, the maximum you are willing and able to pay for one obreros unit is 14 dineros, but you want to pay a lower price if you can. Make a deal with an obrero owner.	You are a producer of ropas. You want to buy six units of obreros. Considering the demand for your product, the maximum you are willing and able to pay for one obreros unit is 5 dineros, but you want to pay a lower price if you can. Make a deal with an obrero owner.
Plato Producer	**Ropa Producer**
You are a producer of platos. You want to buy six units of obreros. Considering the demand for your product, the maximum you are willing and able to pay for one obreros unit is 12 dineros, but you want to pay a lower price if you can. Make a deal with an obrero owner.	You are a producer of ropas. You want to buy six units of obreros. Considering the demand for your product, the maximum you are willing and able to pay for one obreros unit is 4 dineros, but you want to pay a lower price if you can. Make a deal with an obrero owner.
Plato Producer	**Ropa Producer**
You are a producer of platos. You want to buy six units of obreros. Considering the demand for your product, the maximum you are willing and able to pay for one obreros unit is 10 dineros, but you want to pay a lower price if you can. Make a deal with an obrero owner.	You are a producer of ropas. You want to buy six units of obreros. Considering the demand for your product, the maximum you are willing and able to pay for one obreros unit is 3 dineros, but you want to pay a lower price if you can. Make a deal with an obrero owner.
Plato Producer	**Ropa Producer**
You are a producer of platos. You want to buy six units of obreros. Considering the demand for your product, the maximum you are willing and able to pay for one obreros unit is 8 dineros, but you want to pay a lower price if you can. Make a deal with an obrero owner.	You are a producer of ropas. You want to buy six units of obreros. Considering the demand for your product, the maximum you are willing and able to pay for one obreros unit is 2 dineros, but you want to pay a lower price if you can. Make a deal with an obrero owner.

Activity 4
Dineros

12 dineros	12 dineros
12 dineros	12 dineros
12 dineros	12 dineros
12 dineros	12 dineros
12 dineros	3 dineros

LESSON SIX
WHAT (AND HOW MUCH) SHOULD GOVERNMENT DO?

INTRODUCTION

Government plays a role in all economies, but a much larger role in some economies than in others. In a pure command economy, all economic activity would be directed by government planners. Government would make all decisions involving what, how, and for whom to produce, and would own all property. In a pure market economy, economic activity would be organized through markets with a very limited role for government. In reality, how much governments do falls somewhere between these two extremes. Each society ultimately determines the size and scope of markets and how government functions in its economy.

CONCEPTS

Role of government
Command economy
Market economy

CONTENT STANDARDS

There is an economic role for government to play in a market economy whenever the benefits of a government policy outweigh its costs. Governments often provide for national defense, address environmental concerns, define and protect property rights, and attempt to make markets more competitive. Most government policies also redistribute income.

BENCHMARKS

In the United States, the federal government collects taxes to provide public goods and services, enforces antitrust laws and regulations to try to maintain effective levels of competition in as many markets as possible; frequently, however, laws and regulations also have unintended effects—for example, reducing competition.

Markets do not allocate resources effectively if (1) property rights are not clearly defined or enforced, (2) externalities (spillover effects) affecting large numbers of people are associated with the production or consumption of a product, or (3) markets are not competitive.

Governments often redistribute income directly when individuals or interest groups are not satisfied with the income distribution resulting from markets; governments also redistribute income indirectly as side effects of other government actions that affect prices or output levels for various goods and services.

OBJECTIVES

♦ Students identify the six basic functions of government.

♦ Students describe the different roles for government in market and command economies.

♦ Students analyze the costs and benefits of government involvement in command and market economies.

LESSON DESCRIPTION

Students receive cards that describe either a personal goal or a broad social goal that, to some degree, involves a role for government. They trade cards in an attempt to obtain one for which they agree with the government program or level of government involvement. Through discussion, the cards are used to identify the functions of government and to analyze the costs and benefits of government programs in command and market economies.

TIME REQUIRED

Two class periods.

MATERIALS

• Sticky notes, one per student

- Index Cards, one for each pair of students with a function of government written on each card
- Visual 1: Functions of Government
- Visual 2: Government's Share of GDP for Selected Countries
- Activity 1: Trading Cards with cards cut apart
- Activity 2: Retrieval Chart, one per student

PROCEDURES

1. Prior to teaching this lesson, ask students to keep a diary of their daily events for one day, from the time they wake up until they go to bed.

2. Ask students to list and discuss which of their daily activities are regulated in some way by the government, and which goods or services they use that are provided by government. List the responses on the board. *(Answers will vary but could include regulations related to food they consume, taxes they pay – such as sales, income, and social security or FDIC taxes – the school they attend, school buses, driver's licenses, roads and bridges, the minimum wage law, etc.)* Ask students if they know other individuals whose lives are affected by other kinds of government programs. To develop this idea, if students do not suggest these programs themselves, ask if they know people who receive food stamps, unemployment benefits, Social Security retirement benefits, Medicare or Medicaid. Point out that during the course of their day a wide range of government programs affects many aspects of their own lives, and the lives of other people they know.

3. Tell students that even in market economies there is a role for government to play whenever the benefits of the government providing additional goods or services outweigh the costs. However, there is often widespread disagreement about the appropriate scope and size of government in a market economy, because people often disagree about the costs and benefits of these programs.

4. On the board or a bulletin board create a Role of Government continuum similar to the one below:

HOW LARGE SHOULD THE ECONOMIC ROLE OF GOVERNMENT BE IN OUR ECONOMY?

Extensive ------------------------------------Limited

5. Give each student a sticky note. Instruct them to write their name on the note and place it on the continuum at the point that best reflects their personal ideas about the role of government in the economy.

6. Distribute cards from Activity 1. Each card describes either a personal goal or a broad social goal that, to some degree, involves a role for government in the economy. The cards are paired so that statements 1 and 2, 3 and 4, 5 and 6, etc., deal with similar goals or government programs. The cards with odd numbers suggest a more market-oriented approach and limited role for government. The cards with even numbers suggest a more extensive role for government – often to the point of programs associated with command economies and central planning.

7. After distributing the cards, have students read the statement they have been given. Tell them that different cards deal with different personal and social goals for the economy, but each card describes a particular kind of government program and some level of government involvement in the economy. If they agree with the government actions described on the card they received, they should keep that card. If they disagree, they should try to trade the card with another student, to get a card that describes a government program or programs they support.

8. Tell students they have five minutes to make their trades. Conduct the trading period.

Some students may not be able or may be unwilling to make a trade.

9. After five minutes, ask how many students were able to obtain a card describing government programs that they support. Ask them to discuss why it was or was not possible to make a trade.

10. Have the students holding cards with paired numbers (that is, cards 1 and 2, 3 and 4, 5 and 6, etc.) sit or stand together and answer these questions:

A. How do government programs help or hurt people or the nation in terms of achieving the goal that is listed on your card?

B. What are some costs and benefits of the government programs described on each card?

11. Display Visual 1 and distribute a copy of Activity 2 to each student. As each role for government is discussed, have students record how that role is handled on the even number cards under the column labeled Economy A, and on the odd number cards under the column labeled Economy B. Briefly define the functions of government. For each function ask students:

A. What are some examples where this role of government affects you personally? (Refer students to the list generated from their diaries in Procedure 1.)

B. Which pairs of cards related to this role of government?

C. What goal were you trying to achieve on your card?

D. What kinds of government programs were described on your card?

E. How did those government programs help to achieve the goal on the card, or make it harder to achieve the goal?

Answers:
• Providing **public goods** and services – Goods and services that cannot be withheld from those who do not pay for them will not be provided by the private sector because producers know they will not be able to sell these goods or services. Public goods and services are also characterized by shared consumption. Shared consumption means that a good or service can be used by more than one person without reducing the amount of the product available for others to consume.

A. *Examples: National defense and roads*

B. *Cards 11 and 12*

C. *Well maintained super highways*

D. *Market: Use of tax dollars; Command: Planners decide the relative importance of roads, national defense, etc.*

E. *Market: Government uses tax dollars to build and maintain roads, and to provide for national defense; Command: These programs are part of the overall plan setting production goals for all kinds of goods and services.*

• Correct for externalities – Governments can use tax policies, regulations and subsidies to correct for the overproduction or underproduction of goods and services.

A. *Examples: Pollution controls, public education, health service*

B. *Cards 3 and 4, 5 and 6*

C. *Clean air and clean water*

D. *Market: Regulation and fines, licenses to emit some pollution; Command:*

Production methods set by the central plan will entail some level of pollution – often higher than in market economies because of differences in property rights, political structures, and income levels.

E. ***Market***: *Pollution abatement achieved through regulations, fines, or government sales of pollution permits;* ***Command***: *The level of pollution abatement depends on the relative importance of this goal to planners, and the overall level of resources in the economy.*

- Maintain competition – In market economies, governments enforce antitrust laws in an attempt to maintain effective levels of competition in as many markets as possible. Competition among sellers results in lower costs and prices, higher product quality, and better customer service. If one producer can produce total market output for a product at a unit cost that is lower than the cost incurred by two or more producers, competition may not be possible. When this occurs, government may establish regulations to control price, output, and quality. In command economies, the state owns major industries and sets prices for output. Typically there is no direct competition, and goods are produced by a few, very large enterprises.

   A. *Examples: Competition in retail industries; antitrust cases in the computer software industry; command economy giants, such as the Aeroflot airline system in Russia.*

   B. *Cards 1 and 2, 9 and 10, 17 and 18*

   C. *Purchase jeans, insure a company's competitiveness in the marketplace, freedom to open new business*

   D. ***Market***: *Government encourages competition;* ***Command***: *Competition does not exist.*

E. ***Market***: *Individuals are free to open new businesses and businesses are free to organize in ways to lower production costs and increase productivity. Some people lose jobs and some businesses fail.* ***Command***: *Firms do not compete because production output and prices are determined by planners; jobs are guaranteed resulting in employment of more workers than necessary, creating inefficiencies and increased costs of production; state-owned enterprises are not allowed to fail and have "soft" budget constraints.*

- Establish legal framework – Government establishes a society's legal framework through laws that define property rights. Property rights include physical capital and the right to use, develop, and transfer it; and the freedom to earn income, to invest in one's skills, to change jobs, and to spend, save, and raise financial capital.

   A. *Examples: Choose own career path, select type of post-secondary education, choose type of job and place of employment*

   B. *Cards: 13 and 14, 15 and 16, 17 and 18, 21 and 22*

   C. *Buy and sell a house, attend college, select a career, open a business, find good jobs*

   D. ***Market***: *No government programs, government enforces property rights;* ***Command***: *Government does not allow ownership of property, and may limit choice or availability of jobs or careers.*

   E. ***Market***: *By maintaining property rights, the government gives individuals the freedom to buy and sell houses, select careers, determine type of post-secondary education, if any, change jobs, receive rewards for work in the* *form of higher wages and other benefits, and start a business. This results in some people earning and owning more than others. **Command:** Property rights very limited. Individuals do not own homes or land, or open businesses, and are limited in educational and career choices.*

• Income redistribution – Government redistributes income through taxation, spending and assistance programs, and programs that provide training for workers and encourage private investment in education.

A. *Examples: Social security benefits, Medicare, Medicaid, unemployment compensation, government job training programs*

B. *Cards 19 and 20, 27 and 28*

C. *Care for the poor and elderly, adequate and affordable health care*

D. ***Market:** Taxes fund Medicare, Medicaid, job training, social security;* ***Command:** Guaranteed jobs, retirement benefits, inexpensive or free housing; national health care available to all*

E. ***Market:** Social security provided for elderly and disabled, health care available to individuals who meet federal guidelines, limited low-income housing available but long waiting lists. Some individuals cannot afford medical insurance and do not have incomes high enough to afford even the most basic health care. Individuals who apply and qualify receive Medicaid and Medicare.* ***Command:** Individuals have jobs for life, affordable health care, pensions. Health care not always available when needed because of shortages, job may not be one of individual's choice, housing is provided but often with long waiting periods.*

• Reduce inflation and unemployment (macroeconomic stabilization policies) – The federal or national government's taxation and spending policies and the central bank's monetary policies affect overall levels of employment, output, and prices.

A. *Examples: Federal Reserve raises interest rates to curb inflation, lowers interest rates to promote economic growth and stimulate employment.*

B. *Cards: 7 and 8, 23 and 24, 25 and 26*

C. *Curb inflation, full employment, promote economic growth*

D. ***Market:** Monetary and fiscal policies;* ***Command:** Planners set prices so there is no officially measured inflation, determine investment levels, and assign jobs.*

E. ***Market:** Federal Reserve monitors prices, rate of economic growth, and unemployment rate, and adjusts policies to maintain stable prices, constant growth and 4-5 percent unemployment rate.* ***Command:** No official inflation or unemployment; growth rates determined by planners, who may limit consumption to allow greater investment.*

12. Tell students that the Activity 2 responses under Economy A reflect the role of government in a market economy. Those under Economy B reflect the role of government in a command economy. Instruct students to label Economy A, Market Economy, and Economy B, Command Economy. Ask students: What are some of the benefits and costs of the various roles for government in the two types of economies? (***Market:** Benefits – individual freedom to make choices; economic growth depends on how much individuals decide to save and invest; private firms and individuals make*

decisions on how much current income to consume and how much to invest for the future; enforcement of property rights; reduction of negative externalities and increase in positive externalities; competitive markets that provide consumers a variety of products at various prices and qualities; provision of some public goods and redistribution of income to some degree; costs – not all individuals earn same income and have equal benefits; some unemployment and inflation; public goods and services may not be as extensive as some individuals would like; **Command:** *Benefits – some level of security in terms of employment, housing, pensions, and education; business fluctuations seldom a problem because total spending tightly controlled and not allowed to get out of line with the economy's capacity to produce; costs – limited private property rights; government controls the level of investment and thus economic growth; consumer wants for goods and services (public and private) often not met; limited competition reduces incentives for employees and managers and results in higher production costs and poorer quality of goods and services.)*

13. Point out that some of the cards represented extreme examples of the roles for government. In the command economy the state owns almost everything and is responsible for everything from providing food, jobs, health care, and housing to air quality. In a pure market economy the role of government is extremely limited. In reality, economies are mixed and the scope of government varies. For example, in some economies, most property is owned by individuals, but the government is responsible for providing many services such as retirement income, day care, the arts, health care, and public education. In others, government owns major industries and directs investment, but many goods and resources are allocated through market prices.

14. Explain that one way of measuring the size of government in an economy is to look at annual government expenditures or revenues as a share of Gross Domestic Product. Display Visual 2. Discuss:

A. Which countries have the lowest government expenditures as a share of gross domestic product? (*Singapore, Venezuela, United States, Australia*) Which have highest G/GDP? (*Netherlands, France, United Kingdom*) How would command economies such as Cuba and North Korea likely fit into this pattern? (*G/GDP is much higher in these countries.*)

B. What is the major source of revenues for governments? (*taxes*)

C. Which countries have the lowest government revenues as a share of gross domestic product? (*Venezuela, United States, Australia, Singapore*) Which have the highest? (*Netherlands, France, United Kingdom, and Czech Republic*)

D. How does a high G/GDP affect individuals' consumption levels and ability to save? (*Restricts both.*)

E. What generalization might be made about countries with high G/GDP? (*More extensive role for government in the economy, higher tax burden for citizens, less capital investment by private firms.*) With low G/GDP? (*Less extensive role for government in the economy, lower tax burden, greater personal saving, more investments in capital goods by private firms.*)

15. Refer to the Role of Government continuum on the board. Write Command under Extensive Role and Market under Limited Role:

HOW LARGE SHOULD THE ECONOMIC ROLE OF GOVERNMENT BE IN OUR ECONOMY?

Extensive Role------------------------Limited Role
(Command)   (Market)

16. Allow students to reposition their sticky notes if they want to. Ask them to defend their positions on the continuum, and discuss their differences of opinion with students who favored much more or less government activity in the economy.

CLOSURE

1. Divide students into pairs. Distribute the index cards which have one of the economic functions of government written on it.

2. Tell the pairs to write the type of economic system they wish to represent, either command-oriented or market-oriented, below the listed function of government.

3. Tell pairs to write a description of a situation involving their assigned role for government in the type of economy they selected on the back of the index card.

4. Collect and redistribute the cards with the students' description facing up. Ask each pair to read the description, then try to identify the role for government, the type of economy depicted, and the costs and benefits of this role for government or lack of it in the economy. Pairs then read the answer on the front of the card. If a discrepancy exists between the answers of the two pairs, ask the class to determine which answer is correct and why.

ASSESSMENT

Write the following assignments on the board. Instruct students to choose and complete one of the assignments.

1. Choose one of the functions of government. Describe how this role is handled in a command economy. Explain how government programs to fulfill this function would affect your life if you lived in a command economy.

2. Pick one of the functions of government. Describe how this role would be fulfilled in a market economy and in a command economy,

and summarize the costs and benefits for these programs for each type of economy.

Visual 1
Functions of Government

Provide Public Goods and Services

Correct for Externalities

Maintain Competition

Establish Legal Framework

Redistribute Income

Reduce Inflation and Unemployment
(Macroeconomic Stabilization Policies)

Visual 2
G/GDP for Selected Countries

Country	Central Government Expenditures as % of GDP (1998)	Central Government Revenues as % of GDP (1998)*
Singapore	17	24
Venezuela	20	17
United States	21	22
Australia	24.5	24
Germany	33	31
Czech Republic	35	33
Spain	36	30
United Kingdom	38	38
France	46	42
Netherlands	47.6	46

*Includes all revenue to the central government from taxes and nonrepayable receipts other than grants.

Source: <u>World Development Indicators 2000</u>, The World Bank.

Activity 1
Trading Cards

1	2
Goal: Purchase a pair of jeans Many styles, brands, prices and quality of jeans available to buy, produced by different firms that compete for consumer dollars.	Goal: Purchase a pair of jeans One style of jeans produced by a state-owned firm, production quotas set by government planners. Jeans often not available in stores, but only on black market at high prices.
3	4
Goal: Clean air Manufacturing and utility companies must reduce pollution or pay fines.	Goal: Clean air Government officials set high production quotas that result in extensive pollution, but later debate lowering production to improve air quality.
5	6
Goal: Clean water Government sells licenses to pollute. Firms buy licenses when the cost of not polluting is higher than the price of the license.	Goal: Clean water Pollution controls adopted only if reducing pollution is an important goal of government officials and economic planners, compared to producing more goods and services at state owned firms.
7	8
Goal: Curb inflation The central bank raises interest rates when it wants to reduce inflation.	Goal: Curb inflation Official prices for goods and services are set by central planners, so there is usually no inflation in the official price level.

From *Focus: Economic Systems*, © National Council on Economic Education, New York, NY

Activity 1 (continued)

9	10
Goal: Maintain a company's competitiveness Some companies "downsize," laying off workers to lower production costs and increase productivity, to compete with other domestic and international firms.	Goal: Maintain a company's competitiveness Downsizing (firing workers) violates central planners' goal of zero unemployment. International trade is discouraged to promote national self-sufficiency, and to eliminate competition from international firms.
11	**12**
Goal: Drive on well maintained super highways New roads built and maintained with tax dollars.	Goal: Drive on well maintained super highways Central planners allocate some resources to road construction and repair, other resources to producing goods and services at state-owned firms.
13	**14**
Goal: Move to a larger home Individuals may buy and sell, or rent or lease houses, land, or apartments.	Goal: Move to a larger home Government builds apartments and provides them to families, based on criteria such as the number of people in the family and how long they have waited for a larger apartment. Individuals are not allowed to buy or sell houses, apartments, or land.

Activity 1 (continued)

15	16
Goal: Attend college and study geology Individuals can apply to any college or university, and choose their own major. Students must pay tuition.	Goal: Attend college and study geology Government planners determine how many students to admit in different majors at colleges and universities. The government pays tuition for students who are accepted in the schools.
17	**18**
Goal: Open a new business Entrepreneurs are free to buy, rent, and organize resources to open new businesses.	Goal: Open a new business Large state-owned factories produce most products. Government planners decide whether to build new factories or create new firms.
19	**20**
Goal: Care for poor and elderly Tax revenues used to provide food stamps, Medicare, Medicaid, job training, social security benefits. Many workers have a private pension and/or some savings.	Goal: Care for poor and elderly The government guarantees medical care, pensions, and housing for all citizens.
21	**22**
Goal: Good jobs Freedom to choose job and change jobs if dissatisfied. Good work rewarded with higher wages and other benefits. Some people earn more than others.	Goal: Good jobs Most jobs pay similar wages, set by state planners. Limited freedom to move and change jobs without government approval for the new job, housing, etc.

From *Focus: Economic Systems,* © National Council on Economic Education, New York, NY

Activity 1 (continued)

23	24
Goal: Avoid unemployment Unemployment of 4-5 percent considered full employment because of workers changing jobs. Monetary and fiscal policies used to stimulate economy if unemployment goes higher.	Goal: Avoid unemployment Everyone is assigned a job, so no official unemployment exists. Some jobs are maintained where little of value is done, to keep everyone employed.
25	26
Goal: Encourage economic growth Monetary and fiscal policies used to keep growth steady from year to year. Most investments in new factories, machinery, and technology carried out by private firms, funded by private savings.	Goal: Encourage economic growth Central planners determine investment levels, and state-owned firms are expected to achieve these goals. Investments are funded by planners allocating more resources to produce capital goods (used in production), and fewer resources to produce consumer goods.
27	28
Goal: Adequate health care for citizens At the market price, health care services and treatments available for those who can afford to pay. Not all individuals have health insurance from private firms.	Goal: Adequate health care for citizens Health care provided for citizens but long waiting lists for many treatments and services.

Activity 2
Retrieval Chart

Role of Government	Economy A	Economy B
Provide Public Goods and Services		
Correct for Externalities		
Maintain Competition		
Establish Legal Framework		
Redistribute Income		
Reduce Inflation and Unemployment		

LESSON SEVEN
SHADY CREATURES AND THE PROBLEM OF SPECIAL INTEREST GROUPS

INTRODUCTION

Both market economies and command economies face serious political and economic problems arising from special interest groups. In democratic market economies, such as the United States and Canada, most political decisions are made through the legislative process. Special interest groups regularly try to influence legislative decisions – for example, the American Medical Association closely follows and testifies before Congress on legislation affecting health care. In command economies that are not democratic, such as Cuba and China (although China has adopted many market-oriented economic reforms in recent years), most political decisions are made by a small group of powerful party leaders and then implemented through a process of central planning. Special interest groups have considerable influence in these systems, too. For example, the managers of large, state-owned enterprises in China lobby the leaders of the Chinese Communist Party to continue the extensive state subsidies that keep their factories operating.

This lesson uses public policies dealing with international trade to illustrate the problems that can arise from special interest groups. The benefits of free trade are widely acknowledged by the vast majority of economists and by most of the nations of the world community. However, many nations adopt policies that restrict trade. Using fictional nations and products, the main activity in this lesson demonstrates why special interest groups can be

so successful and difficult to control, even though they benefit small groups of people and impose costs on many more people.

CONCEPTS

Benefits of trade

Restrictions on trade (tariffs, nontariff barriers, import quotas, voluntary export restrictions)

Public choice theory

Special interest groups

CONTENT STANDARDS

Costs of government policies sometimes exceed benefits. This may occur because of incentives facing voters, government officials, and government employees, because of actions by special interest groups that can impose costs on the general public, or because social goals other than economic efficiency are being pursued.

BENCHMARKS

Incentives exist for political leaders to implement policies that disperse costs widely over large groups of people and benefit relatively small, politically powerful groups of people.

Although barriers to international trade usually impose more costs than benefits, they are often advocated by people and groups who expect to gain substantially from them. Because the costs are typically spread over a large number of people who each pay only a little and may not recognize the cost, policies supporting trade barriers are often adopted through the political process.

OBJECTIVES

♦ Students recognize how voluntary exchange typically benefits both buyers and sellers, and how free trade among people in different nations benefits both importing and exporting nations by improving standards of living.

♦ Students analyze the economic incentives that make it possible for special interest groups to play an important political and economic role in different kinds of economic systems, including democratic market economies.

LESSON DESCRIPTION

A trading simulation is first used to demonstrate the benefits of free trade. In a later round trade is restricted, which helps a small group of people but hurts many more. Students use basic arithmetic to see why it would be in the economic interest of the small number of people to support the trade restrictions, but not in the interests of most other people to spend much time, effort, or money to actively oppose the trade barriers. Other examples of special interest issues in different types of economies are then discussed.

TIME REQUIRED

One or two class periods.

MATERIALS

- Visual 1: Restrictions on Trade
- Visual 2: What Is a Special-Interest Problem?
- Activity 1: Shady Trading Part 1 – one copy for each student
- Activity 2: Hollywood Squares – copy and cut up enough squares to give one-fourth of the class five squares, and one-fourth of the class 10 squares. Optional: print the five squares that will be given to one-fourth of the class in the second trading round on colored paper, or mark those bills with a special stamp, signature, or some other identifying mark
- Activity 3: Shady Money – copy and cut up enough bills to give one-half of the class an average of eight bills
- Activity 4: Shady Trading Part 2
- Small prizes for the trade simulation that begins with Procedure 3

PROCEDURES

1. Explain to the class that neither market nor command economies operate perfectly. The same is true for political systems. As Winston Churchill once said, "Democracy is the worst system in the world, except compared to everything else." One of the most important and enduring reasons for these failures is the ability of special interest groups to influence public policies, including economic policies. For example, special subsidies for agricultural producers – such as grain, dairy, and tobacco farmers – have been provided in the United States and many other nations for the past 50 years. Today, most economists feel there are no compelling reasons to provide special subsidies to agricultural producers, and no reason to help them instead of producers of clothing, automobiles, entertainment services, or most other goods and services. But farm lobbies have considerable political influence in the United States (where a large number of Senate races are affected by agricultural issues) and in many other nations of the world, such as France and Japan. In the United States, the result of this influence has been that agricultural subsidies have continued under many different presidents, regardless of whether a majority of members of Congress have been Democrats or Republicans. (Many U.S. agricultural subsidies have been reduced sharply in the past 20 years, however.) Special interest groups are also important in the command and transition economics. For example, in China and Cuba managers of state-owned enterprises lobby the government and communist party officials to provide subsidies that will cover their financial losses – in other words, to let them face "soft" rather than hard budget constraints.

2. Explain that the basic purpose of this lesson is to demonstrate why political leaders sometimes choose economic policies that will, over the long run, reduce a nation's overall standard of living. In particular, the lesson shows why a nation might choose to restrict international trade, despite the well known

From *Focus: Economic Systems*, © National Council on Economic Education, New York, NY

benefits of free trade to both importing and exporting nations.

3. Distribute Activity 1 to the class. Allow a few moments for students to read it. Briefly review the story of the alien abduction and the economic situation on SHADE.

4. Announce that the class will play a game in which students take the roles of various citizens of SHADE. Half the class will be sellers of Hollywood Squares and half the class will be buyers of Hollywood Squares. Divide the class into four groups, and tell students that each groups represents a certain sector on the planet SHADE.

A. **Sellers**: Give each student in sectors 1 and 2 five Hollywood Squares (from Activity 2). Tell these students their goal is to sell as many Hollywood Squares as possible at the best possible price. The students who sell their squares at the highest prices will win a small prize.

B. **Buyers**: Give each student in sectors 3 and 4 a supply of Shady dollars (from Activity 3), and explain to the entire class that this is the money used on SHADE. Distribute different amounts of Shady dollars to each buyer so that some students have two or three dollars, and some have five or six dollars, but the average is about four dollars. Tell the buyers their goal is to purchase as many Hollywood Squares as possible at the lowest possible prices. The students who buy their squares at the lowest prices will win a small prize.

5. Allow about three minutes for trading. Have the students move around the room and make as many exchanges as they can. When the time expires, have students return to their seats. Give prizes to the buyer(s) who bought at the lowest prices, and to the seller(s) who sold at the highest prices.

6. Discuss what happened during the first trading round. Ask: How many people made trades? Describe the trades you made. (*Most will have traded. When students describe their transactions, stress the idea that both sides expected to gain from the transaction.*)

7. See if there is consensus about the usual or average price for Hollywood Squares in this trading round. List several prices on the chalkboard. Try to reach consensus on the usual or average price, but do not take the time to calculate the actual average price for all trades. Write the consensus price on the board. Also record the highest and lowest prices at which trades were made.

8. Announce that after a year or two of free trade, the sellers from sector 2 convince the Supreme Shady Creature that people in sector 1 were selling "inferior" Hollywood Squares. The Supreme Shady Creature announced minimum quality standards for Hollywood Squares, and decreed that no sales of squares from sector 1 would be permitted. Collect all of the squares and currency used in round one, and pass out five new squares to the students in sector 2, but not sector 1. You may want to use squares printed in a different color, or marked with your signature, a special stamp, or some other identifying mark in the second trading round. Pass out a new supply of currency to the students in sectors 3 and 4. Make sure that the same total amount of currency is distributed for round 2 as in round 1, but it is not necessary for each student to receive the same amount of currency he or she received in the first trading round.

9. Conduct the second trading round. Explain that in this trading round, citizens of sectors 2, 3, and 4 may trade as before. However, the citizens in sector 1 may not participate. Some students may protest the decision of the Supreme Shady Creature, arguing that this restriction will result in no income for the people in sector 1 and that fewer squares will be available for the buyers in

sectors 3 and 4. Some students may even predict that the average price for a Hollywood Square will increase. Ignore any such protests at this time and conduct the second trading round. Once again, allow about three minutes for trading.

10. After the second trading round, have students return to their seats. Award prizes for the seller(s) who received the highest prices and the buyer(s) who paid the lowest prices.

11. Discuss what happened during the second trading round. Ask: What prices did the sellers charge? (*Again, list several prices on the chalkboard. Try to reach consensus on the usual or average price, but do not take the time to calculate the actual average price for all trades. Write the consensus price for the second trading round on the board, and the highest and lowest trading price, next to the prices for the first round.*)

12. Compare the prices in the two trading rounds. Ask: Why did prices increase? (*The restriction on the citizens of sector 1 reduced the supply of Hollywood Squares. Demand remained unchanged, so the average price should have increased.*)

In which trading round were the Shady creatures better off? (*In the first trading round more sellers earned income, more Hollywood Squares were bought and sold, and buyers were able to buy at lower prices, so most Shady creatures were better off then. In the second trading round the sellers from sector 2 received higher prices, so they were better off. But the people in sectors 1, 3, and 4 were worse off.*)

13. Explain that this trading game illustrates an important principle of economics: Voluntary exchange occurs when all participating parties expect to gain. This is true for trade among individuals or organizations in the same nation, or from different nations, or even different planets. Free trade increases material standards of living. The benefits of free trade are not a secret. They have been long recognized by economists and most world leaders, including all U.S. presidents (Democrats and Republicans) who served during the past 50 years. Free trade within the United States (interstate commerce) is established in the U.S. Constitution.

14. Explain that the widespread knowledge of the benefits of free trade raises an interesting question. If leaders around the world know that open trade improves living standards, why do governments place restrictions on trade? Nearly every nation of the world—including major trading nations such as the United States and the United Kingdom—have adopted different kinds of legal restrictions on trade. Display Visual 1 to illustrate some of the common forms of trade restrictions. Note that there are sometimes national defense reasons for protecting a domestic industry from international competition – e.g., a large nation such as the United States with a major military presence in the world may choose to insure that there is a strong domestic steel, oil, or computer industry. But most trade restrictions are passed for other reasons that have to do with special interest groups, not national or international security issues.

15. Tell the class that some basic arithmetic will demonstrate more clearly why nations adopt trade restrictions even in cases where trade barriers reduce the national standard of living. Distribute Activity 4 to the class. Explain that the circumstances described in this activity are slightly different from those observed in the earlier trading activity. Specifically, to make the SHADE economy somewhat more realistic, we now assume that there are both producers and consumers of Hollywood Squares in each of the four sectors of SHADE. We also increase the total amount of production and consumption, to reflect levels for the entire planet of SHADE. Read over Parts 1 and 2 of Activity 4 together. Then divide the class into pairs and have students work through the questions at the end of the Activity. When all or most of the students have

completed their work, discuss the answers.
Ask:

A. How many squares were sold each year in SHADE when there was free trade? *(100,000 squares)*

B. How many squares were sold after the production from sector 4 was eliminated? *(The three remaining producers could produce and sell 75,000 squares.)*

C. What kind of trade barrier was the decision to eliminate the production from sector 4? *(A nontariff barrier.)*

D. What was the total revenue received by producers in all four sectors before the production from sector 4 was eliminated? *(100,000 squares × $1 dollar = $100,000)*

E. What was the total revenue for producers from sectors 1, 2, and 3 after the production from sector 4 was eliminated? *(75,000 squares × $3 dollars = $225,000)*

F. How much additional revenue did the producers in sectors 1, 2, and 3 receive after the production from sector 4 was eliminated? *(The average price for a square increased by $2 dollars. Therefore, 75,000 squares × $2 dollars = $150,000 in additional revenue for all three producers.)*

G. How much additional revenue did each of the individual producers in sectors 1, 2, and 3 receive as a result of eliminating the production from sector 4? *(The average price increased by $2 dollars, and each producer made 25,000 squares. Therefore, the average revenue for each producer in sectors 1, 2, and 3 increased by $50,000.)*

H. How much more do the Shady creatures who consume Hollywood Squares pay after the production from sector 4 is eliminated, for the total number of squares purchased by all consumers? *(The price increased by $2 dollars; $2 dollars × 75,000 squares = $150,000. In other words, the additional money received by the remaining producers is the additional amount that consumers paid.)*

I. How much is the average (per creature) increase in the amount spent for squares to a Shady creature buyer after the production from sector 4 is eliminated? *(The average price for squares increased by $2 dollars, so those who buy a square pay $2 more than they did before. However, some Shady creatures who bought squares at a price of $1 will not be willing or able to buy a square at a price of $3. After all, there are 100,000 potential consumers, but now production is only 75,000 squares. Some students may subtract the spending for those who can no longer purchase the squares, and therefore calculate the average increase in the amount spent as $150,000 divided by 100,000 potential buyers = $1.50 increase for each potential buyer.)*

J. If you were a producer of squares from sector 1, 2, or 3, what would you be willing to spend to lobby for the trade restriction against the producer in sector 4? *(Probably up to $49,999, but offers are likely to start at a lower level.)*

K. If you were an individual buyer of squares, what would you be willing to spend in time and money to lobby against the trade restriction that eliminates production in sector 4? *(Probably nothing. Individual buyers have relatively little to gain – only $1.50 to $2.00. Most consumers won't be* *willing to spend much time or money fighting the trade restriction.)*

16. Display Visual 2. Explain that most trade barriers adopted by nations reflect special interest problems. Ask: Who could obtain large benefits from restricting production/imports on SHADE? *(The producers from sectors 1, 2, and 3 stand to gain a great deal from the policy restricting production/exports from sector 4.)*

Who bears the costs of the production and trade restriction? *(Buyers of Hollywood Squares. But while the total cost to buyers was high, those costs were spread out over a large number of potential buyers. Therefore, each individual buyer was only hurt a little.)*

17. Explain that special-interest effects often lead nations to impose trade restrictions that hurt their own consumers, or to use tax revenues collected from the general population to support a small group of people or firms. For example, governments in nations that are members of the European Union have quadrupled subsidies to European farmers over the past 20 years. These subsidies cost European taxpayers an estimated $45 billion a year. Less than 5 percent of the population in the nations of the European Union are engaged in farming; but because those benefits go to such a small group of people, they have strong financial incentives to work for the continuation of these programs.

18. Remind the class that both market economies and command economies face problems that arise from special interest groups. Democratic market systems are susceptible to the influence of interest groups. For example, the American Association for Retired Persons (AARP) is the largest organization of midlife and older persons in the United States, with more than 30 million members. AARP's members are known as informed voters. AARP uses its influence to shape government policies affecting such programs as Medicare and Social Security that benefit its members, but the costs of funding such programs are widely diffused across millions of employer and employee taxpayers. Different kinds of examples of special-interest programs are usually found in command economies that are not democratic. For example, in Cuba the economy is directed by central planning. But the managers of large, state-owned factories and enterprises act in much the same way as special interest groups in market systems. For example, they often try to restrict competition from self-employed workers in Cuba. In 1996, one way they did that was to support the introduction of new taxes on self-employed workers. Those taxes led to a large decrease in the number of self-employed workers, from 208,000 in January 1996 to 155,000 in July 1998. Stress how, in this case, the small number of large state enterprises received large benefits by reducing competition, but thousands of self-employed workers and Cuban consumers of the products they produced were hurt.

Conclude by observing that while democratic market systems are not perfect in terms of eliminating special-interest effects, freedom of speech, freedom of the press, and democratic political institutions may make it easier to identify and eliminate or prevent special-interest problems. Have students discuss or debate the following paraphrase of Winston Churchill's observation about democracy (see Procedure 1): "Market economies are the worst economic systems in the world, except compared to everything else."

CLOSURE

Pose the following questions for review. Ask:

1. What usually happens when nations are allowed to trade freely? *(Production levels and living standards increase. There is more competition. Consumers pay lower prices.)*

2. What are some examples of trade restrictions? *(Tariffs, quotas, voluntary export restrictions, other nontariff barriers.)*

3. What creates a special-interest problem? *(When the benefits of a program are highly concentrated, some people or firms have strong incentives to lobby for the program, but the costs of the program are so widely dispersed that most people and firms have no strong incentive to lobby against the program. In other kinds of special interest problems, costs are highly concentrated but benefits are widely dispersed. For example, pollution restrictions or controls on midwest electric companies that burn coal impose high costs on those firms, but the benefits of less pollution are widely dispersed among the millions of people who live in the Northeastern United States and Canada. That means the midwest utility companies have strong incentives to lobby against pollution controls, but the individuals who live in the northeast have only weak incentives to lobby for the controls.)*

4. Can special-interest problems exist in both command and market economies? *(Yes.)*

ASSESSMENT

Ask students to visit the web page of the American Coalition for Ethanol (ACE) at www.ethanol.org (or any similar kind of group with a legislative agenda dealing with a particular product or industry). Tell students to read the Mission Statement, Legislative News, and list of ACE members. Have students write a paragraph that explains how the production of ethanol in the United States is evidence of a special interest group in action in a market economy. Ask:

1. Who benefits from ethanol subsidies?

2. What evidence do you find to suggest that ethanol producers have strong incentives to lobby for the program?

3. Who bears the costs of ethanol subsidies?

Next have students discuss where they could look to find evidence of special interest groups in a command economy, such as Cuba or North Korea. Do students believe that it would be difficult to find such information and act on it? Have students write a paragraph indicating whether they believe it would be more difficult to eliminate special interest problems in a market or command economy, and why.

Visual 1
Restrictions on Trade

Tariffs: Taxes on imported products.

Quotas: Limits on the amount of a product that can be imported.

Voluntary Export Restrictions (VERs): Limits adopted on the amount of products to be exported from one nation to another. VERs are usually adopted by an exporting nation to prevent an importing nation from adopting tariffs, quotas, or other trade restrictions on these products.

Other Nontariff Barriers: Restrictions such as required import licenses, or inspection certificates of product quality (including safety standards), are required before products may be imported.

From *Focus: Economic Systems*, © National Council on Economic Education, New York, NY

Visual 2
What Is a Special-Interest Problem?

Situations that provide large benefits to a relatively small group of people or firms, but spread the cost across a large number of people or firms. (For example, subsidies to grain, dairy, and tobacco farmers.)

Or, situations that impose high costs on a relatively small group of people or firms, but spread the benefits across a large number of people or firms. (For example, pollution control regulations raise costs for a few large firms, but the benefits of a cleaner environment affect millions of people.)

Special-interest groups only consider the high benefits they will receive, or the high costs they will pay – not the overall benefits and costs of the programs. As a result, many nations end up with too many agricultural subsidies, and too much pollution.

Activity 1
Shady Trading: Part 1

The Abduction

You have been abducted by aliens from the planet SHADE (Supreme Headquarters of Alien Development of Earth) located in a far away galaxy. Much to your surprise, the aliens have been friendly to you, and you like them, too. Now they are asking you to help them understand a big problem they are having with their economy. To understand the problem, you will participate in two demonstrations of the SHADE economy. The first demonstration shows the way their economy used to work. The second shows the way it works today. Try to help the Shady creatures throw some light on their problems.

Trade in the SHADE

The creatures of SHADE don't have to spend much for food, clothing, or shelter. But their lives were very boring until they started watching fragments of television broadcasts they received from earth a few years ago. Now they find happiness by buying and selling Hollywood Squares. Some Shady creatures are buyers, and others are sellers. Buyers try to buy Hollywood Squares at low prices, and sellers try to sell them at high prices.

Hollywood squares fade quickly, so a square purchased in one trading period will disappear by the next trading period.

The planet of SHADE is divided into four sectors, similar to what earthlings call nations. In the first period all Shady creatures will trade freely with one another, but the Supreme Shady Creature can regulate inter-sector trade.

The money on SHADE is called Shady dollars.

After each trading round, the Supreme Shady Creature will award small prizes to the best traders – both buyers and sellers. The rewards will go to the sellers who negotiate the highest prices, and to the buyers who negotiate the lowest prices. Stealing and other illegal dealings involving Hollywood Squares are severely punished by sending people out in the dark, where there is no SHADE.

The only legal way to obtain Hollywood Squares is through voluntary trade, at prices negotiated by buyers and sellers.

From *Focus: Economic Systems*, © National Council on Economic Education, New York, NY

Activity 2
Hollywood Squares

Hollywood Square	Hollywood Square	Hollywood Square
Hollywood Square	Hollywood Square	Hollywood Square
Hollywood Square	Hollywood Square	Hollywood Square
Hollywood Square	Hollywood Square	Hollywood Square
Hollywood Square	Hollywood Square	Hollywood Square
Hollywood Square	Hollywood Square	Hollywood Square
Hollywood Square	Hollywood Square	Hollywood Square
Hollywood Square	Hollywood Square	Hollywood Square
Hollywood Square	Hollywood Square	Hollywood Square
Hollywood Square	Hollywood Square	Hollywood Square

Activity 3
Shady Dollars

1 Shady Dollar	1 Shady Dollar	1 Shady Dollar
1 Shady Dollar	1 Shady Dollar	1 Shady Dollar
1 Shady Dollar	1 Shady Dollar	1 Shady Dollar
1 Shady Dollar	1 Shady Dollar	1 Shady Dollar
1 Shady Dollar	1 Shady Dollar	1 Shady Dollar
1 Shady Dollar	1 Shady Dollar	1 Shady Dollar
1 Shady Dollar	1 Shady Dollar	1 Shady Dollar
1 Shady Dollar	1 Shady Dollar	1 Shady Dollar
1 Shady Dollar	1 Shady Dollar	1 Shady Dollar
1 Shady Dollar	1 Shady Dollar	1 Shady Dollar

Activity 4
Shady Trading: Part 2

Directions: Read the following information, then answer the questions that follow.

Part 1: Production of Hollywood Squares
The creatures of SHADE live in four different sectors. Each sector produces and consumes Hollywood Squares, a product enjoyed by almost all Shady creatures. At first, there is free trade in SHADE, which means that Shady creatures from all four sectors are free to make voluntary trades to buy and sell what they wish. Here is some additional background information about trade on SHADE.

- There is 1 producer of Hollywood Squares in each sector, or a total of four producers.

- Each producer makes 25,000 squares per year. The producers cannot expand their production at this time, nor can squares be imported from other planets.

- In all four sectors, there is a total of 100,000 potential buyers of Hollywood Squares.

- Producers are able to sell the 100,000 squares they produce each year at an average price of 1 Shady dollar for each Hollywood Square.

Part 2: The Problem
The Head Shady Creatures (governors) of sectors 1, 2, and 3 convince the Supreme Shady Creature that the producer of Hollywood Squares in sector 4 is producing squares that do not meet quality standards. As a result, the Supreme Shady Creature orders that no Hollywood Squares may be produced in sector 4.

The best Shady economists estimate that the reduction in supply from sector 4 will cause the price of Hollywood Squares to go up by at least one Shady dollar, and perhaps as much as three Shady dollars. That assumes that the producers in sectors 1, 2, and 3 will not increase the price so much that some squares will not be sold. In other words, all of the squares that are produced are expected to be sold at an average price of about three Shady dollars, once the production from sector 4 is eliminated.

Activity 4 (continued)

Questions for Discussion

A. How many squares were sold in SHADE before the production from sector 4 was eliminated?

B. How many squares were sold after the elimination of production from sector 4?

C. What kind of trade barrier was the decision to eliminate the production from sector 4?

D. How much total revenue did the producers in all 4 sectors receive before that restriction was placed on sector 4?

E. How much total revenue did the producers in sectors 1, 2, and 3 get after the restriction was placed on sector 4?

F. How much additional revenue did the producers of sectors 1, 2, and 3 obtain after the restriction was placed on sector 4?

G. How much additional revenue did each producer of sectors 1, 2, and 3 obtain after the restriction was placed on sector 4?

H. How much was the total extra cost Shady creatures paid for the squares after the restriction was placed on sector 4?

I. What was the average (per creature) price to a Shady creature for the purchase of squares after the restriction was placed on sector 4?

J. If you were a producer of squares in sectors 1, 2, and 3, what would you be willing to spend to lobby for the trade restriction against the producer in sector 4?

K. If you were an individual buyer of squares, what would you be willing to spend in time and money to lobby against the trade restriction in sector 4?

LESSON EIGHT
CENTRAL BANKING WITH OR WITHOUT CENTRAL PLANNING

INTRODUCTION

Will Rogers once said, "There have been three great inventions since the beginning of time: Fire, the wheel, and central banking." Although central banking is a far more recent discovery than fire and the wheel, its importance became evident and more widely understood over the past century, especially after such events as the Great Depression, the abandonment of the international gold standard and a global system of fixed exchange rates in the 1970s, and the inflation and other financial crises that occurred during the transition of the economies of the former Soviet Union, Central and Eastern Europe, and the Baltic States from command to market-based economies in the 1990s. The importance of the political independence of central banks from a nation's executive and legislative branches of government has also attracted considerable attention in recent years, because there appears to be a direct relationship between the degree of independence and the level of inflation in different nations.

CONCEPTS

Inflation
Monetary policy
Central bank

CONTENT STANDARDS

Federal government budgetary policy and monetary policy conducted by central banks (in the United States, the Federal Reserve System) influence the overall levels of employment, output, and prices.

BENCHMARKS

In the long run, inflation results from increases in a nation's money supply that exceed increases in its output of goods and services.

Monetary policies are actions taken by central banks (in the U.S. the Federal Reserve System) that lead to changes in the supply of money and the availability of credit.

OBJECTIVES

◆ Students will define inflation, monetary policy, and central bank.

◆ Students will describe the relationship between money supply increases and the rate of inflation.

◆ Students will identify the basic functions of central banks.

◆ Students will analyze the relationship between central bank independence and inflation.

LESSON DESCRIPTION

Students participate in an auction to see how large increases in the money supply can cause inflation. Then they examine data on the relationship between inflation and growth rates in the money supply in different countries. That leads to a discussion of central banks and monetary policy. Finally, students plot a scatter diagram to investigate the relationship between the political independence of central banks in different nations and historical data on inflation in those nations.

TIME REQUIRED

One to two class periods.

MATERIALS

- two bags of candy, raisins, or small foodstuffs – each with the same amount
- Visual 1: Inventions
- Visual 2: Functions of Central Banks

- Visual 3: Inflation and Money Supply Growth Rates, 1987-1997
- Visual 4: Central Bank Independence and Inflation, 1973-1997
- Visual 5: Central Bank Independence and Inflation Graph
- Visual 6: Money Supply Growth Rates and Inflation in Transition Economies
- Activity 1: Smackeroos, enough copies cut apart so that each student receives first a one- and then a three-smackeroo bill
- Activity 2: Central Bank Independence and Inflation, one copy for each student

PROCEDURES

1. Tell the class that it is sometimes claimed that nations could eradicate many social ills, such as poverty, homelessness, and starvation, if only they had more money. Announce that you will conduct a simulation to determine if such social ills could be remedied by printing and distributing more money to everyone in the economy.

2. Show the students the first bag of candy, raisins, or other food items, and explain that you will sell the bag at auction. Announce that the only acceptable "coin of the realm" for the auction will be smackeroos, and give each student a one-smackeroo note. Conduct the auction. Collect the one Smackeroo notes and give the winning bidder the bag. (Note: The price of the bag of candy will be more than one smackeroo if a group of students pools money to purchase the bag.) Write the final auction price and the number of items in the bag on the board, flipchart, or overhead projector.

3. Hold up the second bag of candy, tell the class that it has exactly the same number and kind of items in it as the first bag, and announce that you are going to conduct a second auction to sell this bag. This time give each student a three-smackeroo note. Conduct the auction, write the winning price and the number of items

in the bag below the similar information for the first auction, and discuss the following:

4. How much candy was available for people to buy in the first auction? (*one bag with __ pieces*) In the second auction? (*one bag, also with __ pieces*)

A. Why did the price increase in the second auction? (*Students had more money to spend.*)

B. Did giving each student more money in the second round increase the amount of candy or other items available? (*No more food was available — only more money.*)

C. What happened when the amount of goods and services stayed the same, but the amount of money increased? (*The price increased.*)

5. Point out that simply printing more currency or putting more money into an economy does not guarantee more production and consumption of goods and services. When the amount of money in an economy increases much faster than the level of goods and services produced, that leads to inflation. Define **inflation** as an increase in the general price level of an economy. Note that this does not mean that all prices are going up. For some products that experience decreased demand (such as fashions that go out of style) or decreases in production costs (such as personal computers over the past 20 years) prices may be decreasing. But during a period of inflation, the average level of prices for all goods and services is increasing.

6. Explain that inflation is considered generally detrimental to an economy. Actually, unexpected changes in the price level hurt some groups of people and help others. For example, unexpected inflation hurts people on fixed incomes and people who have loaned out money at fixed interest rates, but helps those who have

borrowed money at fixed interest rates. In that sense, inflation redistributes income, rather than reducing overall real income. But when price levels are stable, people and businesses don't have to spend time and effort to look for ways to protect their incomes and investments from inflation or deflation. That is how price stability improves the overall climate for investment, economic growth, and economic security in an economy.

7. Point out that despite the advantages of price stability, inflation has been a serious problem in various times and places throughout history, including the Roman Empire, Spain and England during the sixteenth century, the colonies during the American Revolutionary War, in the United States (and especially the Confederacy) during the Civil War, Germany during the 1920s, the United States and many countries of South America during the 1970s, and the transition economies of the former Soviet Union, Central and Eastern Europe, and the Baltic states during the 1990s. Today, many nations use central banks to try to reduce inflation and maintain price stability. Explain that a **central bank** is established by a national government to conduct **monetary policy**, which means controlling the amount of money and the availability of credit in the economy. The price of money and credit is, of course, the rate of interest. Therefore, as central banks increase or decrease the supply of money and the availability of credit, interest rates will tend to decrease or increase, respectively. Point out that there were only 18 central banks in different countries of the world at the beginning of the 20th century, but by 1999 almost every country in the world had a central bank. The current central bank of the United States, the Federal Reserve System, was established by legislation passed in 1913. (For more information and activities on "the Fed," see the NCEE's Focus: High School Economics, or an economics textbook.)

8. Display Visual 1. Guide students to the idea that a key role of central banks is to control the supply of money and the availability of credit in an economy, to prevent inflation or deflation. (**Deflation** refers to falling average price levels, which occurs when the production of goods and services increases sharply faster than the amount of money in the economy. Like inflation, deflation helps some groups of people and hurts others, and it is probably not as conducive to the overall investment climate and level of economic security in a country as a stable price level – one with neither sharp inflation or deflation.)

9. Display Visual 2 and review the key functions of most central banks:

A. **Conduct monetary policy** – Central banks have considerable control over a nation's money supply, interest rates, and the availability of credit. Statistics indicate that economies with the highest sustained growth rates in their money supply also have the highest inflation. Display Visual 3, and let students discuss the individual data points and the general relationship between these 10-year averages for rates of inflation and rates of growth in the money supply for these nations. If necessary, ask students whether higher growth in the money supply seems to lead to higher rates of inflation, especially at very high (over 20 percent a year) rates of growth in the money supply, which clearly exceed any realistic rate of growth in a nation's output of goods and services. (*Yes, as the average money growth rate increases, the inflation rate tends to increase.*) Point out that the challenge for central banks is to increase the money supply enough to facilitate economic growth without creating inflation or deflation.

B. **Act as the national government's bank** – Many nations in the world use their central banks as the fiscal agent for their national government. In the United

States, the Federal Reserve System processes U.S. government checks and food stamps. Most central banks buy and sell government securities because when they purchase government bonds with money that increases the amount of money in the economy (because the bonds purchased with money are not widely accepted as payment for purchases). Conversely, when central banks sell government bonds, that decreases the amount of money in the economy. Therefore, trading government securities becomes a key tool of monetary policy for central banks. Many central banks also issue currency. The U.S. currency, Federal Reserve Notes, is distributed by the Federal Reserve through commercial banks. (The currency is printed for the Federal Reserve by the Bureau of Engraving and Printing at the U.S. Treasury.)

C. **Serve as bankers' bank** – Most central banks accept deposits from commercial banks and provide checks or other asset clearing services when deposits are shifted from bank to bank. In the United States, the Federal Reserve's 12 district banks process millions of checks that are drawn on accounts at commercial banks from all around the nation. Checks are cleared in a matter of days, even if they are sent thousands of miles away from the area where the person who writes the check has his or her checking account. An electronic payments system is used to transfer balances from banks where checks are drawn to banks where checks are deposited by the people, businesses, or agencies who accepted the check as payment for goods and services.

D. **Regulate banks** – In some countries, the central bank regulates banking practices and supervises banks to ensure that they are operated safely. In the United States,

the Federal Deposit Insurance Corporation that guarantees deposits up to $100,000 is not part of the Federal Reserve System. However, the Federal Reserve System does regulate many aspects of commercial bank operations, and some activities of banks and other financial institutions, such as margin requirements for purchasing stocks.

10. Remind students that the key role of central banks in most countries today is achieving price stability (i.e., avoiding inflation or deflation) through appropriate monetary policies. But that raises a question: If central banks can eliminate inflation using monetary policy, why do some countries have more inflation than others? Explain that there are many factors, but one factor that has become increasingly apparent is the independence of central banks from executive and legislative branches of government. Such independence allows central banks to pursue monetary policies that will prevent or reduce inflation, even when those actions are unpopular with political leaders or the public at large. To explore this topic, begin by considering why certain kinds of monetary policies could be unpopular.

11. Read students the following scenario: In the year 2012 inflation is a serious problem in the U.S. economy, so the Federal Reserve System tightens the money supply and reduces the availability of credit, which causes interest rates to rise. Meanwhile, the country's president, Jacqueline F. Roosevelt, all of the House of Representatives, and a third of the Senate are running for re-election.

12. Have students speculate on the results of the new monetary policy. (*The higher interest rates will probably lead to less borrowing and spending in the economy, and the unemployment rate may rise. Specific examples will vary, but some possibilities: People will buy fewer homes and cars. Home and auto sales will fall. Some*

carpenters and autoworkers will lose their jobs. Sales of lumber and steel will decrease, so more people will lose their jobs). Will the president and members of Congress who are running for reelection like this policy? *(Some candidates may, if they are in districts where voters are very concerned about the effects of inflation. But in general, unless inflation is severe, voters tend to be unhappy with political incumbents when unemployment is rising and the economy is slowing down. The monetary policies can therefore create a problem for the political incumbents, and many if not most would be happier if the Federal Reserve System had not tried to fight inflation this way, especially during an election year.)*

13. Explain that the U.S. Federal Reserve System, like many central banks in the most prosperous market economies of the world, has a high degree of independence from the executive and legislative branches of government. The Governors of the Federal Reserve are appointed for long, staggered, terms, and the Federal Reserve earns enough money by charging for the services it provides to commercial banks and others that it does not request operating funds from the federal government. Usually the situation is quite different for central banks in command economies, where government planners also determine monetary policies. There are also some market economies where central banks are largely controlled by the executive and/or legislative branches of national government.

14. Ask students to consider why an independent central bank may be a good idea. *(As shown above, elected officials have some reasons not to support tight monetary policies that fight inflation. They also have incentives to increase spending programs – especially in their own districts – that can increase inflationary pressures in the economy. Central bank officials who are not elected and not under the direct control of elected officials are in a better position to hold the line against inflation, even if it requires actions that are not politically*

popular at the time. They are also under less pressure to create or print new money to fund government borrowing for new programs, which increases inflationary pressure in the economy.)

15. Display Visual 4, and ask students if these data support the idea that central banks that are more independent are more effective in fighting inflation. Explain that the first column reports the average annual inflation rate for each country from the years 1973 to 1997. The second column represents a measure of central bank independence developed by several economists, in which higher numbers represent a greater degree of independence. Distribute a copy of Activity 2 to each student. Read the instructions, and have students complete Activity 2.

16. Display Visual 5, and ask how their Activity 2 straight lines slope. *(Downward.)* What do these data and graphs suggest about the relationship between inflation and central bank independence? *(There is a negative relationship - more independence is associated with lower inflation, and vice versa.)* Point out that this is only a correlation, and correlation does not prove causation. In other words, there may be other explanations of why some nations have lower inflation, but several studies have supported the idea that greater independence of the central bank is associated with lower inflation. That statistical correlation appears to occur for the reasons discussed above - greater independence allows central bankers to fight inflation more aggressively, even when doing so is not politically popular.

17. Display Visual 6, and explain that this table shows average money growth rates and inflation in economies that are moving away from command and towards market-based economies. Point out that the average inflation rate (i.e., increase in price level) for industrialized countries was approximately 2.2 percent during the same time period. Have students speculate on the degree of central bank independence in these countries, noting that

these countries had been command economies as a part of or associated with the former Soviet Union. Ask students how high rates of inflation could affect the transitions toward market economies for these countries.

CLOSURE

Review the main points of the lesson.

1. Inflation is an increase in the general price level.

2. Inflation is directly related to increases in the money supply.

3. Central banks are created by governments in most nations to conduct monetary policy.

4. Monetary policies are actions of the central bank that affect the money supply, interest rates, and the availability of credit in an economy.

5. The more independent a nation's central bank is from political control and pressure, the lower the inflation rate in the nation tends to be.

ASSESSMENT

Explain that the command economies of the former Soviet Union had a difficult time making a transition to independent central banking after the collapse of communism in the early 1990s. The International Monetary Fund and the World Bank encouraged the development of strong central banks that would control inflation.

These policies were politically unpopular, because standards of living were already low in these nations, compared to Western market economies, and the "tight money" policies, when combined with the movement away from large state-owned factories and enterprises, resulted in levels of unemployment that had never been experienced during the last decades of the Soviet period.

Finally, have students explain Visual 6, and identify the three countries that are most likely to have independent central banks. Students should explain their choices.

From *Focus: Economic Systems*, © National Council on Economic Education, New York, NY

Visual 1
Inventions

"There have been three great inventions since the beginning of time: fire, the wheel, and central banking."

Will Rogers

Visual 2
Functions of Central Banks

- ## Conduct monetary policy

- ## Act as the national government's bank

  - serve as depository for funds
  - issue checks for the government
  - buy and sell government securities

- ## Serve as bankers' bank

  - accept deposits from banks
  - provide check clearing services, and transfer bank funds to reflect deposits and withdrawals from accounts at different banks

- ## Regulate some transactions at banks and other financial institutions

From *Focus: Economic Systems*, © National Council on Economic Education, New York, NY

Visual 3
Inflation and Money Supply Growth Rates, 1987-1997

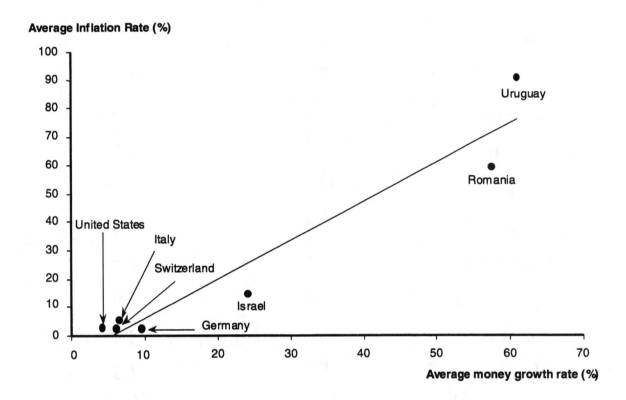

Source: *International Financial Statistics Yearbook*, International Monetary Fund, Washington D.C., 1999.

Visual 4
Central Bank Independence and Inflation, 1973-1997

Country	Average Inflation	Index of Central Bank Independence
Australia	6.8	2.0
Belgium	4.9	2.0
Canada	5.5	2.5
Denmark	6.2	2.5
France	6.5	2.0
Germany	3.5	4.0
Italy	11.1	1.8
Japan	3.6	2.5
Netherlands	3.8	2.5
New Zealand	8.9	1.0
Norway	6.4	2.0
Spain	10.5	1.5
Sweden	10.7	2.0
Switzerland	3.4	4.0
United Kingdom	8.4	2.0
United States	5.0	3.5

Sources: Patricia Pollard, "Central Banking Around the World," Federal Reserve Bank of St. Louis, 1998, derived from Alberto Alesina and Lawrence H. Summers, "Central Bank Independence and Macroeconomic Performance: Some Comparative Evidence," *Journal of Money Credit and Banking*, (May 1993), pp. 151-162. *International Financial Statistics Yearbook*, 1999.

Visual 5
Central Bank Independence and Inflation Graph

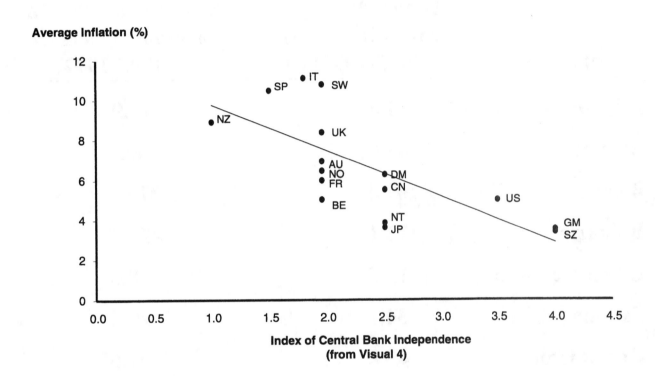

Average Inflation (%)

Index of Central Bank Independence
(from Visual 4)

Visual 6
Money Supply Growth Rates and Inflation in Transition Economies

Country	Average Annual Money Growth Rate (%) (1995-1997)	Average Increase in Consumer Prices (%) (1995-1997)
Albania	41.4	17.9
Armenia	41.6	69.5
Belarus	107.4	275.3
Bulgaria	173.1	422.5
Czech Republic	13.5	8.8
Estonia	34.7	20.8
Kazakhstan	45.8	77.6
Latvia	11.7	17.0
Lithuania	19.8	24.4
Poland	31.7	21.0
Romania	80.8	75.3
Russia	56.7	86.5
Slovak Republic	14.3	7.3
Ukraine	61.4	157.6

Source: International Financial Statistics Yearbook, 1999.

Activity 1
Smackeroos

1 Smackeroo 1	3 Smackeroo 3
1 Smackeroo 1	3 Smackeroo 3
1 Smackeroo 1	3 Smackeroo 3
1 Smackeroo 1	3 Smackeroo 3
1 Smackeroo 1	3 Smackeroo 3
1 Smackeroo 1	3 Smackeroo 3

Activity 2
Central Bank Independence and Inflation

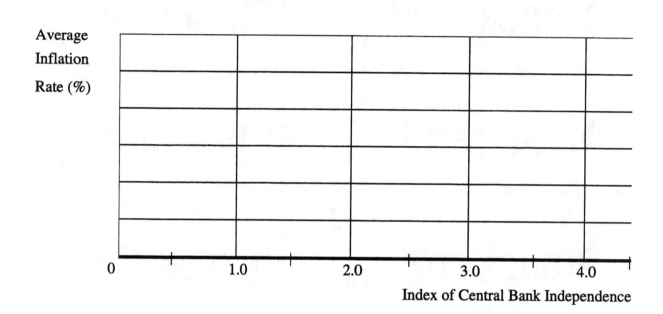

Average
Inflation
Rate (%)

0   1.0   2.0   3.0   4.0

Index of Central Bank Independence

1. Scale the vertical axis on the left in increments of 2 percentage points, from 0-12%.
2. Plot a scatter diagram using the data from Visual 4, *Central Bank Independence and Inflation, 1973-1997*. Label each point with the name of the country. (Use small letters! You may want to print the name in a blank space and draw an arrow to the data point for that country.)
3. Start on the inflation axis and moving right, draw a single **straight** line that comes as close as possible to all of the points you have drawn.
4. What does the line you drew suggest about the relationship between the two variables listed on the axes for this graph: central bank independence and inflation?

LESSON NINE
THE MYSTERIES OF UNEMPLOYMENT: HOW CAN YOU HIDE SOMETHING SO MACRO?

INTRODUCTION

In a market system employers are willing to pay higher wages and salaries to employees who can produce more or better goods or services in a given amount of time. Labor productivity depends upon the worker's training and skills, technology, and the efficient use of other productive resources or inputs.

Unemployment occurs when some people who are actively looking for jobs are not able to find work. Underemployment occurs when workers have jobs that do not allow them to work as many hours as they want, or jobs that do not fully use their training and skills. Unemployment and underemployment affect levels of national income (GDP) and economic growth. International comparisons of unemployment rates must be used with caution because of differences in how employed and unemployed workers are counted. In many command economies, although full employment is achieved by providing jobs for all workers, there is extensive underemployment and "hidden" unemployment.

CONCEPTS

Labor force
Labor productivity
Unemployment
Underemployment

CONTENT STANDARDS

A nation's overall levels of income, employment, and prices are determined by the interaction of spending and production decisions made by all households, firms, government agencies, and others in the economy.

Investment in factories, machinery, new technology, and the health, education, and training of people can increase labor productivity and the standard of living.

Unemployment imposes costs on individuals and nations.

BENCHMARKS

Labor productivity is measured by dividing the amount of output produced by the amount of labor used to produce it.

Unemployment exists when people who are actively looking for work do not have jobs.

When unemployment exists, an economy's production is less than its potential GDP and some labor resources are not used.

OBJECTIVES

♦ Students define labor force, productivity, and unemployment.

♦ Students explain how the labor force, productivity, and unemployment are measured.

♦ Students compare different production situations to determine what factors affect labor productivity.

♦ Students simulate underemployment and describe its effects on productivity and official measures of employment and unemployment.

LESSON DESCRIPTION

Students learn how economists measure the labor force, unemployment and labor productivity and see how international differences in national employment goals and procedures for measuring unemployment can make it difficult to compare the performance of different economic systems. Students then participate in a classroom simulation to experience some of the causes and effects of underemployment.

TIME REQUIRED
Two class periods.

MATERIALS
- Activity 1: If the (Labor) Force Is With You, You Count, one copy for each student
- Activity 2: It Takes More Than Labor to Get the Job Done, one copy for each student
- Activity 3: The Queue Blues at the Central Store, copies of pages: Security Guard (1), Cashier (1), Clerk (6), Customer (1 for every remaining student), Qblue Currency and Customer ID (1/customer), Official Security File (3), Food Receipts (1/customer), Master Account Sheet (1 for every 4 customers), Food Items (1 for every 4 customers) (Optional) Scissors, 5 pair, if Central Store employees are cutting forms

PROCEDURES
1. Give each student a copy of Activity 1. Explain that unemployment rates are ratios or fractions, comparing the number of people (16 or older) who want to work and are actually looking for work but do not have jobs (the numerator) with the number of people who want to work and are actively looking for or have jobs (the denominator). Explain that the denominator measures what economists call the **labor force**, and the numerator measures the number of people who are in the labor force but **unemployed**. By definition, an unemployed person must be a member of the labor force and thus actively seeking work. Individuals who are retired, institutionalized (e.g., in prison), or who choose not to work for whatever reason are **not** counted as unemployed, because they are not counted as part of the labor force.

Have students complete the computations and questions for the two cases described in Activity 1. Discuss the following answers with the class:

Case 1: *(Initially employed = 100, unemployed = 25, unemployment rate = 25/125 =1/5 or 20 percent); (After the lottery, employed = 100, unemployed = 20, unemployment rate = 20/120 = 1/6 or 17 percent)*

What conclusions can you draw from this example? *(Even when the number of jobs remains the same, the unemployment rate will change if the size of the labor force changes. The same number of people (5) was subtracted from both the numerator and denominator, resulting in a smaller fraction or ratio.)*

Case 2: *(Initially employed = 70, unemployed = 30, unemployment rate = 30/100 or 30 percent); (After the new government policy is adopted, employed = 100, unemployed = 0, unemployment rate = 0 percent)*

What conclusions can you draw from this example? *(Unemployment rates do not measure how productive workers are. If production levels remain the same but more people are employed, employment rises and unemployment falls. But **productivity** or output per worker is also lower.)* Tell students that this is one way that official measures of unemployment can be reduced in command economies, creating what some market economists have called "hidden" or "disguised" unemployment.

2. Give each student a copy of Activity 2. Explain that worker productivity is affected by many factors. Instruct students to write a paragraph summarizing a real world situation in which they observed worker productivity to be high, medium, or low. They should list changes in the process that might raise or lower productivity. Have students summarize to small groups or to the class as a whole what they wrote.

3. Announce that students will now participate in a simulation, called "The Queue Blues at the Central Store." Assign eight employee roles, distribute the employee role-playing pages (with six different clerk roles circled) and a customer role page to each remaining student. Allow time for students to sign and read their pages. Then explain the following rules for the simulation.

Eight students are employees at the Central Store. One is the security guard, who monitors store traffic and disruptions. One is the cashier, who handles all the cash transactions. The remaining six employees are counter clerks who process orders for one of three food items. Make sure the six clerks write their names at the top of their role cards. One of those six students is assigned to each of the following jobs:

Chicken order clerk
Chicken distribution clerk
Bread order clerk
Bread distribution clerk
Milk order clerk
Milk distribution clerk

All of the remaining students will take the role of customers. Give each customer a sheet with the identical amount of currency (7 Qblues), and one official Customer ID card, which must be signed before the simulation begins.

4. Set up three separate food counters in the "store," as far apart as possible (perhaps in corners of the room) and tell the order and distribution clerks for each food to staff their counters. Give each of the three order clerks an Official Security File.

Check that the order clerks at each counter know the price for their product: Chickens cost 2 Qblues, milk and bread cost 1 Qblue.

Give the chicken and bread distribution clerks two times the number of chicken and bread food units as there are customers in the simulation. Give the milk distribution clerk as many milk units as there are customers.

5. Provide the Security Guard with some type of "official" identification (a headband, armband, badge or other insignia). Instruct the Guard to stand at the store entrance/exit at the beginning and end of the simulation, and to patrol the store while transactions are made.

6. Set up a separate location for the cashier, as far away from the counters as possible. Give the Cashier the Master Account Sheets to record all cash transactions for food items purchased in the store. Give the cashier twice as many chicken and bread receipts as there are customers, and one milk receipt for each customer. (Provide scissors to the security guard, cashier and distribution clerks if you want them to cut the forms apart.)

7. Be sure students understand their roles and the rules of the Central Store before the purchases begin. (The rules should result in a slow pace and low levels of productivity. But they reflect the way stores were often run in the former Soviet Union (FSU).) Most of the eight employees will be idle much of the time, waiting for transactions to be processed. Customers will spend a lot of time waiting in lines. Do not allow the participants to change or eliminate any of the required steps. People in the FSU often spent most of their day off shopping in many stores that operated with these rules, which was one cost of the procedures designed to provide jobs for everyone on the one hand, and to mask persistent shortages of consumer goods on the other hand. (See the discussion of these points in the introductory essay by George Horwich.)

8. Once the eight store employees are in position, begin the simulation by allowing customers to pass the entry checkpoint. Tell the Security Guard to be certain that each customer has a signed Customer ID.

9. Time is an important element in measuring the labor productivity of this exercise. Record the total time it takes to complete the game, beginning with the first customer entering the security checkpoint and ending when the last customer exits, after all shopping is completed.

10. After completing the simulation, ask students to discuss the experience using the following discussion questions:

A. How many individual food orders were processed in the simulation? *(There are five units of food on each customer's shopping list, so there are five times the number of customers total transactions. If the cashier was accurate, the Master Account Sheet should match this number.)*

B. Were all employees of the Central Store always busy? If not, who was less busy? (The *milk clerks had fewer transactions than bread or chicken clerks. The Security Guard is less busy in the middle of the activity. The cashier is always busy once sales begin.*)

C. Was the store efficient? *(No.)* What rules created the inefficiency? *(Separate shopping areas, double paperwork, some jobs where workers were often idle.)*

D. Tell the class: "In command economies, full employment is sometimes achieved by hiring more workers than necessary to produce some goods or services, which results in low productivity. That creates one kind of (what economists call) **underemployment**. Were some of the workers at the Central Market underemployed? How could you tell?" *(Yes. Some workers were often idle, or working very slowly.)*

E. Ask: "In any economy, income levels and what people can consume depend upon the level of goods and services produced. Therefore how will unemployment and underemployment affect the standards of living and income levels?" *(Lower them.)*

F. Ask: "Assuming a labor force of eight workers and a work time of ____ minutes (teacher provides this measurement), what was the productivity of the Central Store workers, measured in terms of the number of food orders filled?" *(number of individual food orders from question 10A divided by eight times ___ minutes. For example, if the simulation took 15 minutes, and there were 27 customers, the productivity is: (27 × 5) / (8 × 15) or 1.5 orders per worker minute.)*

G. Ask: "Suppose changes in government regulations and procedures for processing food orders at the Central Store result in significant increases in worker productivity. Compare your first estimate of labor productivity at the Central Store to this new situation, assuming that the same number of individual orders are completed by the eight workers in 10 fewer minutes of labor time. *(Old productivity = (customers × 5)/(8 × __ minutes). New Productivity = (customers × 5)/(8 × ___ -10 minutes).)*

CLOSURE

Read and ask students to comment on the following statement: In market economies unemployment is higher than in command economies, but in command economies there is likely to be more underemployment. There does tend to be more unemployment in market economies – especially during recessions – at least using official definitions and measures of unemployment. But in most periods, most unemployed workers are only "frictionally" unemployed while they change jobs.

From *Focus: Economic Systems*, © National Council on Economic Education, New York, NY

There was so much underemployment in the former Soviet Union that a lot of unemployment was hidden or disguised. Average production and income levels were certainly lower in the FSU, and in many of the command economies that still exist today, than in the industrial market economies. That reflects these kinds of full employment policies as well as differences in property rights and other kinds of institutional policies. It should also be noted that there has been a level of protection from unemployment in the command economies that is not always provided to workers in market economies.

ASSESSMENT

1. Discuss with students why the size of a nation's labor force, and the number of people employed and unemployed, might vary from country to country, or over time in the same country. *(These changes might be triggered by demographic and cultural changes, such as the "baby boom" or the trend of more women taking jobs in the labor market. Differences in government policies, such as minimum wage laws and unemployment insurance, may also have important effects. In the case of transition countries, the change from one economic system to another has also resulted in different patterns of unemployment and underemployment.)*

2. Assign related research projects to teams of students. One team might analyze the data on labor productivity, employment or unemployment from East and West Germany before, during, and after reunification. Another team might analyze data on the former Soviet Union. Another team might compare and contrast several neighboring countries in South America, or the effects of NAFTA on employment and living standards in the United States, Canada, and Mexico.

Activity 1
If the (Labor) Force Is With You, You Count

Definitions:
- **Employed** – adults (16 and over) who have jobs (part-time or full-time).
- **Unemployed** – adults (16 and over) who do not have a job, but have actively looked for work in the past 30 days.
- **Labor force** – all adults (16 and over) who have jobs, or who do not have jobs but have been actively looking for work in the past 30 days. In other words, the labor force is the sum of employed and unemployed.
- **Unemployment rate** - number of unemployed divided by the labor force.

Case 1: The Incredible Shrinking Labor Force

Suppose an economy has a labor force of 125 people and there are currently 100 jobs filled. Determine the number of employed, unemployed, and the unemployment rate.

Now suppose that 5 people who had jobs share a big lottery prize and decide to retire for the rest of their lives. Assuming the same number of jobs are filled after these people retire, compute the number of employed, unemployed, and unemployment rate.

What conclusions can you draw from this example?

Case 2: The Incredible Invisible Unemployment

Suppose an economy has a labor force of 100 people and 70 jobs, with 30 of those jobs in the public/government sector. Determine the number of employed, unemployed, and the unemployment rate.

Suppose the government decides it is unacceptable to have an unemployment rate this high. Officials declare that two workers instead of one will now be hired to fill each of the current 30 government jobs. The amount of work/production done will not change, but two workers will do what was previously done by one worker. Given these changes, recompute the number employed, unemployed, and the unemployment rate.

What conclusions can you draw from this example?

Activity 2
It Takes More Than Labor to Get the Job Done

Instructions: Think about real world situations in which you observe labor producing goods or services. Describe the production process in several sentences and discuss whether labor productivity appeared to be high, medium, or low. What changes in the process might raise or lower the productivity of these workers?

(Example: Chopping vegetables for a large family dinner. Productivity is lower if the tools for chopping are dull. A food processor or electric chopper might increase productivity.)

Activity 3
The Queue Blues at the Central Store

ROLE-PLAYING PAGE

Name _____   Role: Security Guard

In this simulation you will be the Security Guard at the Central Store. All customers who enter must show you their official shopper ID cards. Once in the store, they must stand in lines to select, pay for, and then pick up different food items. They must not create any disturbances while they stand in line and they must pay for whatever they buy. When they leave the store, you must check their ID cards again, and make sure they have the proper receipts for each item they purchased, with the necessary signatures. Any discrepancies in the paperwork are grounds for arrest. The store employees will call you if violations of any rules occur. Arrest any violators, confiscate any food items and money from people you arrest, and hold them in a secure area until the police arrive to take them to jail.

To review, your job is to:

- Check customers' official ID cards for signatures when they enter the Central Store.
- Observe transactions between customers and employees.
- Arrest any customers who violate rules. Confiscate their money and food, and hold them for the police.
- Inspect customers' IDs, receipts, and food items when customers leave the store.

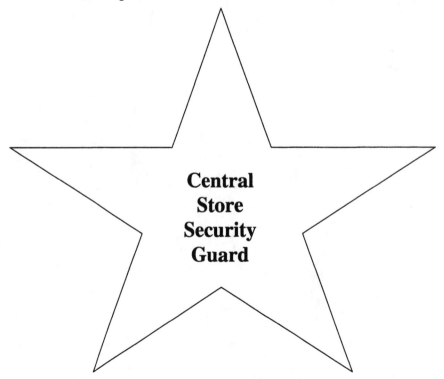

**Central
Store
Security
Guard**

Activity 3 (continued)

ROLE-PLAYING PAGE

Name _____   Role: Cashier

    In this simulation you are the Central Store cashier. Your job is to collect money for food orders placed by customers at different counters in the store. Customers must tell you what item they are purchasing, and pay you the right amount of money. (Each chicken costs 2 Qblues, each loaf of bread or bottle of milk costs 1 Qblue.) When you receive the money, give them one receipt form for each chicken, each bottle of milk, or each loaf of bread that they purchase. Sign the receipt and have the customer sign the receipt. Then have the customers sign the Master Account Sheet for each chicken, each loaf of bread, or each bottle of milk that they purchase, and record the items purchased and the amount of money paid. Then tell the customer to go back to the food counter to pick up the items they purchased.

To review, your job is to:

- Collect the money for each purchase.
- Complete a receipt for each item purchased, with the customers' signature and your signature.
- Have the customer sign the Master Account Sheet for each item purchased and complete the other information on the item purchased and the price paid.
- Send the customer back to the food counter.

Activity 3 (continued)

ROLE-PLAYING PAGE

Name _____

Role: Chicken order clerk
Chicken distribution clerk
Bread order clerk
Bread distribution clerk
Milk order clerk
Milk distribution clerk

In this simulation you will be an order or distribution clerk, as assigned and circled above, at one of the specialty food counters. Sign your name in the space above. You will work with a partner at the counter to process orders.

If you are an order clerk, your job will be:

Tell people who ask what the price is for the product you are selling. When a customer wants to order food at your counter, they must give you their ID card. Do not accept orders from customers who do not have ID cards. The ID cards are placed on the Official Security File sheet until the customer returns with a receipt from the cashier to pick up the order. Keep the Official Security File in a location where you and your partner can reach it. When the customer pays the cashier and returns to your counter with a receipt, your partner, the distribution clerk, will collect the receipt, return the customer's ID card, and give them what they have purchased.

Read the job description below for the distribution clerk to understand how you will work together at your counter.

If you are a distribution clerk, your job will be:

First read the job description of the order clerk, above, to understand how you will work together at your counter. Your job is to give customers who have a payment receipt their ID card and the product they have purchased. Be sure to check the signature on the ID card and their receipt to make sure you are giving the right number of items to the right person. Also make sure that the cashier has signed the receipt. Tear the completed receipt, so that no one else can use the receipt. Keep one half for your records, one half goes to the customer, along with their food item and their ID card.

Cost of food items: Chicken, 2 Qblues; Bread, 1 Qblue; Milk, 1Qblue

Activity 3 (continued)

ROLE-PLAYING PAGE

Name _____   Role: Customer

In this simulation, you play the role of a customer. You will be given 7 Qblues in currency. Your job is to purchase food for your family dinner. Your shopping list is: 2 chickens, 2 loaves of bread, and 1 bottle of milk. To enter the Central Store, you must sign and show your Customer ID to the security guard. Rules must be strictly followed in the store. You will be arrested if you don't observe the rules.

Shopping Rules:

Each food item must be ordered at its own special counter. Go to a counter, give the clerk your Customer ID, find out the price and order what you want. Then you will pay a cashier for the item and get a receipt. Take the receipt back to the counter to get the item you have purchased and your Customer ID. For example, to buy chickens you will:

- Stand in line at the chicken counter.
- Order the chicken and leave your ID with the chicken order clerk.
- Stand in the cashier line, pay for the chicken, and get your receipt.
- Return to the chicken counter with your receipt, stand in line to pick up your chicken and shopper ID.
- If you have more food items on your shopping list, repeat this process.
- When you leave the store, show the security guard your purchases and receipts.

After "leaving the store", you may return to your seat.

Activity 3 (continued)

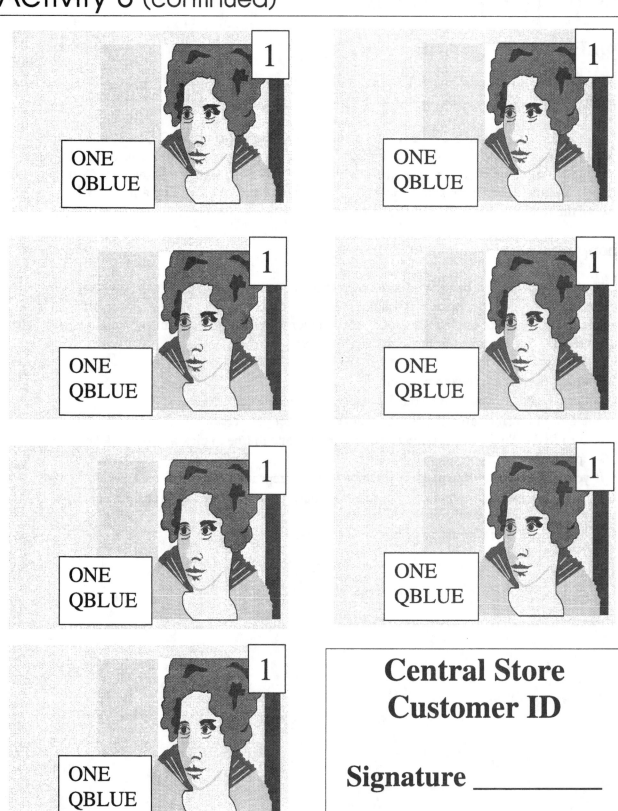

ONE QBLUE 1 (×7)

Central Store Customer ID

Signature _____

Activity 3 (continued)

OFFICIAL SECURITY FILE

Place Customer ID here X	**Place Customer ID here** X
Place Customer ID here X	**Place Customer ID here** X
Place Customer ID here X	**Place Customer ID here** X

Activity 3 (continued)

**BREAD RECEIPT
(1 loaf)**

Customer _____

Cashier _____

**BREAD RECEIPT
(1 loaf)**

Customer _____

Cashier _____

**FOOD RECEIPT
(1 chicken)**

Customer _____

Cashier _____

**FOOD RECEIPT
(1 chicken)**

Customer _____

Cashier _____

**FOOD RECEIPT
(1 bottle of milk)**

Customer _____

Cashier _____

Activity 3 (continued)

MASTER ACCOUNT SHEET
for use by Central Store Cashier
Sheet number ____

	Customer Name		Food	Qblues
	(Print)	Signature	Item	Received
1.				
2.				
3.				
4.				
5.				
6.				
7.				
8.				
9.				
10.				
11.				
12.				
13.				
14.				
15.				
16.				
17.				
18.				
19.				
20.				
21.				
22.				
23.				
24.				
25.				
26.				
27.				
28.				

Activity 3 (continued)

Food Items For Sale to Customers

LESSON TEN
WHY ARE SOME NATIONS WEALTHY?

INTRODUCTION

Some nations have achieved great economic success yet others remain in poverty. To economists, this indicates that different nations have experienced different rates of long-term economic growth. What explains differences in economic growth? Natural resources can be important, of course, as seen in the U.S. experience. Although some nations with few natural resources have achieved high standards of living, some nations that are richly endowed with many natural resources have not. In this lesson, students see that nations that have persistently adopted the basic characteristics of a market economy – institutions that encourage savings and investment, protect private property rights, and promote decentralized decision making rather than central planning – have historically been more likely to enjoy higher growth rates and standards of living.

CONCEPTS

Economic growth
Productivity
Property rights
Saving and investment
Physical capital and human capital
Natural resources
Trade

CONTENT STANDARDS

Investment in factories, machinery, new technology, and the health, education, and training of people can raise future standards of living.

There is an economic role for government to play in a market economy whenever the benefits of a government policy outweighs its costs. Governments often provide for national defense, address environmental concerns, define and protect property rights, and attempt to make markets more competitive. Most government policies also redistribute income.

BENCHMARKS

Economic growth is a sustained rise in a nation's production of goods and services. It results from investments in human and physical capital, research and development, technological change, and improved institutional arrangements and incentives.

Historically, economic growth has been the primary vehicle for alleviating poverty and raising standards of living.

An important role for government in the economy is to define, establish, and enforce private property rights. A property right to a good or service includes the right to exclude others from using the good or service and the right to transfer the ownership or use of the resources to others.

OBJECTIVES

◆ Students predict factors associated with national long-term economic growth.

◆ Students explore the relationship between economic growth and the factors commonly associated with market economies, including property rights; institutions promoting saving and investment in human capital and physical capital; and free trade.

LESSON DESCRIPTION

Students work in pairs to examine data from several nations regarding size, natural resources, and population. Using these data they make predictions about which nations are likely to be below, at, or above the world average of per capita Gross Domestic Product (GDP). GDP is the basic economic measure of national income, so per capita GDP is a key measure of a nation's per person income. Students check their predictions against actual per capita GDP data.

They then review and discuss economists' findings about the factors that contribute most to long-term economic growth.

TIME REQUIRED
One class period.

MATERIALS
- Visual 1: Rating Mystery Nations
- Visual 2: Mystery Nations Revealed
- Visual 3: Factors Contributing to Long-Term Economic Growth
- Activity 1: Mystery Nation Cards, cut apart

PROCEDURES
1. Explain to the class that in this activity they will predict which nations of the world are wealthy and which are not using data on different nations' size, population, and natural resources. Have the students work in pairs. Give each pair a Mystery Nation card cut from Activity 1. Tell the students to read the card and predict whether the nation is below, above, or at the average level of per capita income for all nations of the world. Tell the class that the U.S. Central Intelligence Agency estimated that in 1998 the average level of GDP per capita for all nations of the world was $6,600. Tell the students to place a check mark next to the rating of their choice.

2. Display Visual 1. Record the students' ratings. Once the predictions are recorded, ask some students to explain the reasons for their choices. *(Students often guess that nations A, B, C, D, E, F, H, J, K, L are the wealthiest. Their intuition is usually that large countries with vast stores of natural resources will lead to high levels of income and material wealth. Some students favor nations such as A and K because, in addition to having a large store of natural resources, these nations have a relatively small population.)*

3. Display Visual 2. Discuss how well the students did in estimating the wealth of the Mystery Nations. Students rarely guess that

nations G, I, and M are nations with high levels of income, because of their lack of natural resources and, in the cases of nations G and M, their small size compared to their relatively large populations.

4. Have students suggest answers to the following questions:

A. How can some nations with few natural resources – such as Japan and Singapore – be relatively wealthy?

B. How can other nations with vast amounts of natural resources – such as Russia and Peru – be relatively poor?

5. Explain that some economists call this problem the "natural resources paradox." Natural resources have certainly contributed to the economic success of some nations, including the United States, South Africa, and the oil-rich nations of the Middle East. But there are many examples of nations such as Japan and Hong Kong that have achieved great economic success with relatively few natural resources. And some nations with vast stocks of natural resources, such as Russia, remain relatively poor. In a class brainstorming session, have the students list other factors that might promote or discourage long-term economic growth and high standards of living.

6. Display Visual 3. Briefly review each of the factors that promote long-term economic growth. Here are some of the points that you might highlight.

A. Investments in both **physical capital** (factories and machines) and **human capital** (the health, education, and training of workers) promote long-term economic growth. Both are also related to the widespread use of new technologies, which often require new machinery and training of workers. Over the past two centuries, technological innovations have been the single most important determinant of economic growth, followed closely by investments in physical and human capital. Wealthier nations are usually in better positions to fund additional investments in physical and human capital, but less developed nations often present other kinds of opportunities for new investments. For example, lower levels of incomes mean that labor costs are lower in those nations, and it is often possible to transfer new technologies and production methods from wealthier nations to the poorer nations.

B. Successful economies have institutions that encourage saving and investment. Saving means not spending all of the nation's income for the current consumption of goods and services. Resources that are consumed today can't be used for investment, and vice versa. But successful investments lead to higher future levels of production, income, and consumption. When a business buys new equipment or builds a new factory, it is investing. Some forms of government spending, such as building new roads and bridges, are also investments. Similarly, workers and nations invest in human capital by devoting resources to education and training of current and future workers.

C. In market economies, high after-tax incomes (wages, rent, interest, and profits) represent the major financial incentives that motivate work, saving, and investment. Those incentives also require a strong set of property rights, so that people are able to keep and control the goods and services they purchase with their incomes. Command economies often rely on other forms of incentives, which generally prove to be less effective. However, many of those economies invest heavily in heavy industry and human capital. As a result,

in some decades command economies have grown quite rapidly.

D. A stable currency (low levels of inflation) enhances incentives by maintaining the value of financial assets, which encourages saving and investment. Preventing inflation also keeps people's efforts directed at work, saving, and investing, rather than searching for ways to protect their assets from the effects of inflation.

E. Political instability in a nation makes investment there riskier and leads to lower levels of economic growth.

F. The high income nations of the world are heavily involved in world trade – and in fact, the United States is both the wealthiest nation in the world and the world's largest trader. Canada, Germany, the United Kingdom, Japan, France, Singapore, and Hong Kong are also heavily engaged in international trade. Trading leads nations to specialize in the production and export of the goods and services they can produce at the lowest opportunity cost. Trading those exports for other products that can be produced at a lower cost in other nations reduces the total cost of production and allows higher levels of consumption worldwide. Free trade also results in increased competition, which keeps prices lower for consumers and helps insure that businesses are responsive to consumer demand. Levels of trade have increased dramatically over the past 25 years. As much as one-third of U.S. economic growth during the 1990s has been attributed to the international trade sector of the economy. Nevertheless, international trade is controversial because it adversely affects businesses that must compete with foreign producers.

G. Although moderate population growth and increases in a nation's labor supply promote economic growth, very rapid rates of population growth, such as those observed in many Third World nations over the past 50-75 years, clearly contribute to a vicious cycle of poverty. Such rapid increases in population (when the population doubles in 20 years or less) require higher levels of current consumption for basic food, clothing, and shelter, which lead to lower levels of saving and investment.

H. Point out that, taking all of the earlier factors listed on Visual 3 into account, it is not surprising that market economies have, historically, experienced higher levels of economic growth than command economies (such as Cuba and the former Soviet Union). In market economies, financial incentives to promote work, saving, and investment appear to be more effective than the incentives or punitive disincentives provided under the command economies. That advantage was strengthened even more by greater freedom of choice in consumption and career matters, and by the greater variety of products made available by privately owned, profit-seeking firms. Competition among firms producing similar products also encourages greater efficiency than is achieved in the command economies.

CLOSURE

To review the basic points of the lesson, ask:

1. How important are natural resources to a nation's wealth? *(Natural resources have certainly contributed to the economic success of some nations. But there are many examples of nations and regions such as Japan and Hong Kong, that have achieved great economic success with very few natural resources.)*

2. What are the major factors that encourage long-term economic growth? *(Successful economies encourage greater productivity through investments in physical capital, human capital, and technology; control inflation and maintain political stability; experience moderate but not rapid population growth; encourage international trade; and provide strong financial incentives and protect property rights, which encourage people to work, save, and invest in themselves and in business opportunities. Over the past century, the nations with the greatest economic growth were those that adopted the key characteristics of a market economy.)*

ASSESSMENT

Answer either number 1 or 2.

1. Explain why Japan, with its history of trade barriers and few natural resources, has experienced economic growth.

2. What information do you need to predict the per capita income of a nation?

Visual 1
Rating Mystery Nations

World: GDP per capita: $6,600 (1998 est.)

Mystery Nation A
_____ Below average: per capita income below $6,000
_____ About average: per capita income from $6,000 to $7,000
_____ Above average: per capita income above $7,000

Mystery Nation B
_____ Below average: per capita income below $6,000
_____ About average: per capita income from $6,000 to $7,000
_____ Above average: per capita income above $7,000

Mystery Nation C
_____ Below average: per capita income below $6,000
_____ About average: per capita income from $6,000 to $7,000
_____ Above average: per capita income above $7,000

Mystery Nation D
_____ Below average: per capita income below $6,000
_____ About average: per capita income from $6,000 to $7,000
_____ Above average: per capita income above $7,000

Mystery Nation E
_____ Below average: per capita income below $6,000
_____ About average: per capita income from $6,000 to $7,000
_____ Above average: per capita income above $7,000

Mystery Nation F
_____ Below average: per capita income below $6,000
_____ About average: per capita income from $6,000 to $7,000
_____ Above average: per capita income above $7,000

Mystery Nation G
_____ Below average: per capita income below $6,000
_____ About average: per capita income from $6,000 to $7,000
_____ Above average: per capita income above $7,000

Mystery Nation H
_____ Below average: per capita income below $6,000
_____ About average: per capita income from $6,000 to $7,000
_____ Above average: per capita income above $7,000

Visual 1 (continued)

Mystery Nation I
_____ Below average: per capita income below $6,000
_____ About average: per capita income from $6,000 to $7,000
_____ Above average: per capita income above $7,000

Mystery Nation J
_____ Below average: per capita income below $6,000
_____ About average: per capita income from $6,000 to $7,000
_____ Above average: per capita income above $7,000

Mystery Nation K
_____ Below average: per capita income below $6,000
_____ About average: per capita income from $6,000 to $7,000
_____ Above average: per capita income above $7,000

Mystery Nation L
_____ Below average: per capita income below $6,000
_____ About average: per capita income from $6,000 to $7,000
_____ Above average: per capita income above $7,000

Mystery Nation M
_____ Below average: per capita income below $6,000
_____ About average: per capita income from $6,000 to $7,000
_____ Above average: per capita income above $7,000

Visual 2
Mystery Nations Revealed

World: GDP per capita: $6,600 (1998 est.)

Mystery Nation A: Argentina
GDP per capita: $10,300 (1998 est.)
Rating: Above average

Mystery Nation B: Afghanistan
GDP—per capita: $800 (1998 est.)
Rating: Below average

Mystery Nation C: China
GDP per capita: $3,600 (1998 est.)
Rating: Below average

Mystery Nation D: Cuba
GDP per capita: $1,560 (1998 est.)
Rating: Below average

Mystery Nation E: Egypt
GDP per capita: $2,850 (1998 est.)
Rating: Below average

Mystery Nation F: Ghana
GDP per capita: $1,800 (1998 est.)
Rating: Below average

Mystery Nation G: Hong Kong (Special Administrative Region [SAR] of China)
GDP per capita: $25,100 (1998 est.)
Rating: Above average

Mystery Nation H: India
GDP per capita: $1,720 (1998 est.)
Rating: Below average

Mystery Nation I: Japan
GDP per capita: $23,100 (1998 est.)
Rating: Above average

Mystery Nation J: Nigeria
GDP per capita: $960 (1998 est.)
Rating: Below average

Visual 2 (continued)

Mystery Nation K: Peru
GDP per capita: $4,300 (1998 est.)
Rating: Below average

Mystery Nation L: Russia
GDP per capita: $4,000 (1998 est.)
Rating: Below average

Mystery Nation M: Singapore
GDP per capita: $26,300 (1998 est.)
Rating: Above average

Source: The World Factbook 1999, Central Intelligence Agency website:
www.odci.gov/cia/publications/pubs/html.

Visual 3
Factors Contributing to Long-Term Economic Growth

- Technological innovation (including technology transfers from more developed nations)

- High investment levels in physical and human capital

- Strong incentives to save, invest, and increase productivity (including property rights)

- High rates of savings (to permit high levels of investment)

- Low inflation

- Political stability

- Free trade

- Slower rates of population growth

- Decentralized decision making in most sectors of the economy

Activity 1
Mystery Nation Cards

Mystery Nation A
Area: slightly less than three-tenths the size of the U.S.
Natural resources: fertile plains, lead, zinc, tin, copper, iron ore, manganese, petroleum, uranium
Population: 36,737,664 (July 1999 est.)

Mystery Nation B
Area: slightly smaller than Texas
Natural resources: natural gas, petroleum, coal, copper, talc, barite, sulfur, lead, zinc, iron ore, salt, precious and semiprecious stones
Population: 25,824,882 (July 1999 est.)

Mystery Nation C
Area: slightly smaller than the U.S.
Natural resources: coal, iron ore, petroleum, natural gas, mercury, tin, tungsten, antimony, manganese, molybdenum, vanadium, aluminum, lead, zinc, uranium, hydropower potential (world's largest)
Population: 1,246,871,951 (July 1999 est.)

Mystery Nation D
Area: slightly smaller than Pennsylvania
Natural resources: cobalt, nickel, iron ore, copper, manganese, salt, timber, silica, petroleum
Population: 11,096,395 (July 1999 est.)

Mystery Nation E
Area: slightly more than three times the size of New Mexico
Natural resources: petroleum, natural gas, iron ore, phosphates, manganese, limestone, gypsum, talc, asbestos, lead, zinc
Population: 67,273,906 (July 1999 est.)

Mystery Nation F
Area: slightly smaller than Oregon
Natural resources: gold, timber, industrial diamonds, bauxite, manganese, fish, rubber
Population: 18,887,626 (July 1999 est.)

Mystery Nation G
Area: six times the size of Washington, DC
Natural resources: outstanding deepwater harbor, feldspar
Population: 6,847,125 (July 1999 est.)

Activity 1 (continued)

Mystery Nation H
Area: slightly more than one-third the size of the U.S.
Natural resources: coal (fourth-largest reserves in the world), iron ore, manganese, mica, bauxite, titanium ore, chromite, natural gas, diamonds, petroleum, limestone
Population: 1,000,848,550 (July 1999 est.)

Mystery Nation I
Area: slightly smaller than California
Natural resources: negligible mineral resources, fish
Population: 126,182,077 (July 1999 est.)

Mystery Nation J
Area: slightly more than twice the size of California
Natural resources: petroleum, tin, columbite, iron ore, coal, limestone, lead, zinc, natural gas
Population: 113,828,587 (July 1999 est.)

Mystery Nation K
Area: slightly smaller than Alaska
Natural resources: copper, silver, gold, petroleum, timber, fish, iron ore, coal, phosphate, potash
Population: 26,624,582 (July 1999 est.)

Mystery Nation L
Area: almost twice the size of the U.S.
Natural resources: wide natural resource base including major deposits of oil, natural gas, coal, and many strategic minerals, timber
Population: 146,393,569 (July 1999 est.)

Mystery Nation M
Area: slightly more than 3.5 times the size of Washington, DC
Natural resources: fish , deepwater ports
Population: 3,531,600 (July 1999 est.)

LESSON ELEVEN
NO SACRIFICE IS TOO GREAT FOR SOMEONE ELSE TO MAKE

INTRODUCTION

People in rich and poor countries pollute the environment. So do people in market and command economies. Why? Pollution is encouraged when some of the environmental costs associated with the production or consumption of a good or service can be shifted over to people who do not produce or consume the product. That is true in any nation, and in any kind of economic system. But as pointed out in the introductory essay for this volume, the former Soviet Union and its satellites in Eastern Europe were arguably the "world's worst industrial polluters. . . Because clean air and water are usually public goods that cannot be purchased by consumers in the marketplace, the demand for them in any society can only be expressed in open democratic forums, such as free elections and a free media. These were totally absent in the Soviet Union." (p. 9) In democratic market economies there is certainly some public demand for environmental regulations and clean-up programs, but legislators and ultimately voters have to decide how much regulation and clean-up makes sense.

CONCEPTS

Incentive
Externality

CONTENT STANDARDS

People respond predictably to positive and negative incentives.

There is an economic role for government to play in a market economy whenever the benefits of a government policy outweigh its costs. Governments often provide for national defense, address environmental concerns, define and protect property rights, and attempt to make markets more competitive. Most government policies also redistribute income.

BENCHMARKS

Responses to incentives are predictable because people usually pursue their self-interest.

Externalities exist when some of the costs and benefits associated with production and consumption fall on someone other than the producers or consumers of the product.

OBJECTIVES

◆ Students will define incentives and describe how they direct people's actions.

◆ Students will define externalities and explain why pollution is an example of a negative externality.

◆ Students will understand that the failure to make consumers and producers bear all of the environmental costs associated with the production or consumption of a product will lead to pollution in any kind of economic system.

◆ Students will describe how a tax on pollution can be used to reduce pollution in the economy. They will also understand that it is possible to spend too much or too little to reduce pollution.

LESSON DESCRIPTION

In this lesson, students are engaged in a production simulation that demonstrates different production decisions about the use of resources under different types of economic systems. Students analyze the results of the simulation to discover that the failure to make producers or consumers pay all of the costs of using the environment leads to pollution in all types of economic systems. That establishes an economic role for government, to reduce pollution up to the point where the additional benefits from pollution reduction are no greater than the additional costs of continuing to clean up the environment.

TIME REQUIRED
One class period.

MATERIALS
- Activity 1: Manager Cards, cut apart
- 2 large bags of elbow macaroni and 2 large bags of dried lima beans, mixed together
- three bowls
- box of 30 or more small (bathroom) paper cups
- six sheets of 8 ½ × 11 inch paper
- bag of small candies
- three pairs of scissors
- tape

PROCEDURES
1. Before teaching the lesson, set up three desks/tables in front of the class. On each table, place one manager card (face down) from Activity 1, a bowl of beans and macaroni (mixed together), a stack of 10 or more bathroom paper cups, two sheets of paper placed under the bowl, and a pair of scissors.

2. Tell the class that you want to perform an experiment, and you want three volunteers to serve as managers of factories that produce a food product. Explain that they will each operate a factory that fills and covers paper cups with a macaroni/bean mixture. Show the bag of candy, and announce that managers will be paid pieces of candy if they follow the instructions on their cards. State that you will pay only for full and covered cups. **The managers must pour the food mixture from the bowls into the cups. They may not scoop up the mixture with a cup or with their hands. Any food mixture they touch with their hands can not be counted as production, due to health and safety regulations.** Then they must cut a cover and place it on the top of the filled cup. Hold up one of the manager cards, and emphasize that each manager must pay attention to the

conditions on his or her card. Let the class and the managers know in advance that the three cards are different.

3. Allow time for the managers to read their cards. If they have any questions, have them whisper the questions to you, and be sure to whisper the answers.

4. Give the managers a little time to plan and organize their production. Explain that they may not use anything other than the materials on top of the table. Tell the class to observe the differences in production.

5. Conduct a short production period (about one or two minutes), allowing enough time for Managers 2 and 3 to fill more than six cups. Warn the managers 30 seconds before you stop the production.

6. Announce that you will now pay the managers based on their production and the directions on each of their cards. Remember, only count and pay for full, properly covered cups. Give the appropriate number of candies (maximum six candies) to Manager 1. (This manager will probably have filled exactly six cups, with quite a bit of waste on the table/floor.) Announce how much you pay each of the managers as you pay them. Now pay Manager 2 the base pay of three candies for five cups plus one candy for each cup over five. (This manager will probably have at least five filled cups, and more likely even more, but still with some food spilled on the table/floor.) Pay Manager 3 one candy for each filled cup, but tax the manager one piece of candy for every four inches of tape you are required to use to clean up his or her mess. Do not provide any explanations at this time. (It is most likely that Manager 3 will produce less than Manager 2, because he or she spent time cleaning up spilled food or being more careful not to spill food in the first place.)

From *Focus: Economic Systems*, © National Council on Economic Education, New York, NY

7. Have the managers leave any mess they've made and return to their seats. Discuss the results with the class.

A. Stand at the factory of Manager 1. Have students report their observations about what happened at this company. (*The manager probably filled six cups and then sat down. He or she probably also "polluted" the area around the factory.*)

B. Go to the second factory. Have students report their observations. (*The manager most likely filled five or more cups, and probably had some pollution, but perhaps less than Manager 1.*)

C. Go to the third factory. Have students report their observations. (*The manager probably did not fill as many cups as Manager 2 because he or she either took time to clean up the pollution, or worked more carefully to avoid the pollution in the fist place. In some cases, this manager may have used one of the pieces of paper to make a paper funnel to reduce spilling.*)

8. Define an economic **incentive** as a reward or penalty that people receive for engaging in more or less of a particular activity. Have students discuss and form hypotheses about why the production results might have varied at the three factories, based on the general idea that people respond predictably to economic incentives. Ask students to speculate what kinds of incentives were included on each of the three managers' cards. Then have the managers read their cards aloud to class, and ask the class to identify:

A. What incentive(s) did Manager 1 face? (*a salary for meeting a production quota, and unspecified threats if the quota was not met*) Did Manager 1 have any incentive to avoid making a mess or to clean up the mess? (*No, the manager was paid for six full, covered cups whether there was a mess or not.*)

B. What incentive(s) did Manager 2 face? (*to fill and cover as many cups as possible and receive as much salary plus profit-sharing bonus as possible*) Did Manager 2 have any incentive to avoid making a mess or to clean up the mess? (*This manager's contribution to the firm's profits is made in two ways: 1) producing more output, and 2) minimizing waste. The desire to produce more output may lead to some waste, but the manager has at least some incentive to reduce waste, too, that would show up more in the long run than it may in this one-time simulation.*)

C. What incentive(s) did Manager 3 face? (*to fill and cover as many cups as possible and receive as much salary plus profit-sharing bonus as possible, but avoid or minimize the pollution tax*)

9. Point out that the incentives for Manager 1 are typical of those used in command economies where production quotas are established by the government's central planners. Managers 2 and 3 were operating in a market economy, but there is more environmental regulation facing Manager 3. Point out that a command economy could impose penalties on managers of workers at factories that pollute, if the central planners choose to do so. However, in the former Soviet Union that was rarely done because (as discussed in the Introduction to this volume by George Horwich) that entails lower production levels and higher costs; income levels were low in the former Soviet Union; and the democratic institutions of free elections and a free press to express the demand for a better environment were absent.

10. Explain that the tax on waste created an incentive for Manager 3 to operate the factory more carefully because that company had to

recognize and bear some cost for polluting the environment. For the other companies and managers, pollution costs were ignored, and not paid by either the producers or consumers of the product. That is an example of a negative externality. An **externality** is a cost or benefit associated with production or consumption of a product that "spills over" to a third party – which means people who are not producers or consumers of the product. Have students identify the externality in the simulation. (*Someone else must clean up the food waste created during production.*) Assign and pay two students to clean up the mess created by Managers 1 and 2. (Pay them each one piece of candy.) Discuss the following:

A. Which "third parties" had to bear the cost of the pollution created by Managers 1 and 2? (*the two assigned cleaners and perhaps the "taxpayers" in the class who would ultimately pay their wages*)

B. Does pollution occur because of an economic system of state planning and self-serving bureaucrats (as in the case of Manager 1), or does pollution occur because of an economic system of greedy capitalists (as with Managers 2 and 3)? (*Some pollution probably occurred in both kinds of economic systems. If it didn't occur in your class, point out that in the real world pollution has certainly occurred in both market and command economies. Therefore, the type of economic system does not seem to be the basic reason or cause of pollution.*)

C. Why does pollution occur? (*It occurs most frequently when people are allowed to use the environment without paying for the use of it. That usually happens in the air, oceans, or rivers, because no one owns those resources or has the incentive to make someone who pollutes pay for the damage to the air or water.*

For similar reasons, there is often more trash in public parks than in people's front yards, because no one person owns the public parks and has as much incentive to stop littering there as they do at their own home. The common ownership of air, oceans, rivers, and public parks makes it easier for polluters to shift the costs of cleaning up the pollution onto others.)

D. How can pollution of publicly owned land, water, and air be reduced? (*Fines for littering at public parks are, in effect, a kind of tax on pollution, such as the tax facing Manager 3 in the simulation. Many governments in market economies charge effluent taxes on pollution. That creates an incentive for people and firms to reduce their waste.*)

11. Tell the class that just a few decades ago sewage was dumped into the nearest river in many major U.S. cities. St. Louis dumped its sewage into the Mississippi River until 1967, when it began to use wastewater treatment plants so that cleaner water was returned to the river. Stronger federal and state laws and regulations were adopted to reduce pollution in that period, partly because people became more aware of the health and other costs associated with pollution. But the United States is a wealthy nation, and many studies show that as a nation becomes more prosperous, the public demand for a cleaner environment increases. In poor nations, people are more concerned with finding jobs that pay enough to keep them fed, clothed, and housed, and less concerned with environmental quality.

12. Ask: Is it possible to spend too much to prevent pollution? (*From an economic perspective, the answer is clearly yes. Pollution is costly, but so is reducing pollution. It doesn't make good economic sense to spend more to reduce pollution than the pollution costs in the first place. Typically, removing the first 10 percent of some pollutant from the environment*

is much less expensive than removing the last 10 percent. In other words, the costs of pollution reduction often start out relatively low but rise faster and faster. The benefits of pollution reduction, on the other hand, are usually very high initially, but get lower and lower as the environment gets cleaner and cleaner, and there is less pollution left to harm people, plants, or animals. Therefore, as is often the case in economics, pollution reduction should be carried out only as long as the benefits of any additional reductions and clean-up are greater than the costs.)

13. Conclude by reviewing the idea that people and businesses can have incentives to pollute in any type of economic system – whenever producers and consumers of a product don't have to pay some of the environmental costs associated with making or using the good or service.

CLOSURE

Summarize the lesson by reviewing the following points.

1. What is an economic incentive? *(an additional reward or penalty that people receive for engaging in more or less of a particular activity)*

2. What is an externality? *(a cost or benefit associated with production or consumption of a product that spills over to a third party)*

3. How can environmental pollution be reduced? *(by making producers or consumers bear the environmental cost of making or using products)*

4. Does the type of economic system cause pollution? *(No. Pollution levels increase when the costs of using the environment are ignored. This can happen in a command or a market-oriented economic system. But the lack of democratic political institutions and a free press in the former Soviet Union, together with much*

lower levels of personal income, seem to have led to significantly more severe environmental problems there than were experienced in most industrialized market economies during the same period.)

ASSESSMENT

Have students answer number 1 and/or 2.

1. In many suburban high schools, there are giant parking lots full of automobiles that students drive to school, even though bus transportation is available. Discuss the environmental impact of school policies that allow students to drive to and park at school. Describe the incentives for such actions and the externalities created. Suggest a policy to reduce the environmental problems caused by the current policy, taking care to identify the costs and benefits of both the current and proposed policies.

2. Develop a list of positive and negative incentives for the student body to reduce litter in the school building and on the school grounds

.

Activity 1
Manager Cards

Manager 1

Congratulations! You manage a state-owned factory that produces foodstuffs. To produce one unit, pour the food mix to fill a cup completely to the top and then cover it. Do not touch the top or inside of the cups or the food mix that goes into the cups with your hands. Your quota is six units. There are penalties if you don't meet your quota, but no reward if you produce more than six units. Any food that drops outside of cups is contaminated and cannot be used. You will have about one minute to complete your production, and your cups must be arranged in a straight line (like this: OOOOOO) before you begin to fill them. After you fill your cups, you must place a square paper cover over the food. Each corner of the square must just touch the edge of the cup. When the production period begins, fill the six cups and cover them as quickly as possible. Sit down as soon as you're finished. You'll be paid one piece of candy for each cup you produce, up to six pieces. You're only paid for six cups, so don't waste your time filling any more. The sooner you get those cups filled, the sooner you can begin your vacation!

Manager 2

Congratulations! You have just been promoted to plant manager at the Fill-'Er Up Food Company. All those years of hard work have paid off! Now you will earn a higher salary and share in the company's profits. Your factory fills and covers cups with foodstuffs. To produce one unit, pour the food mix to fill a cup completely to the top and then cover it. Do not touch the top or inside of the cups or the food mix that goes into the cups with your hands. Any food that drops outside of cups is contaminated and cannot be used. Fill as many cups as possible in the production period, which will last about one minute. The money the company gets from selling the cups pays for raw materials, labor, plant and equipment. After those expenses are paid, what's left is profit. You will receive a base salary of three pieces of candy if you fill at least five cups. You will receive this base salary as long as you have this job. Your share of the profits will be one piece of candy for each cup filled after you have filled five cups. (For example, if you fill eight cups, you will receive three additional candies.) Your cups must be arranged in a straight line (like this: OOOOOO) before you begin to fill them. After you fill your cups, you must place a square paper cover over the food. Each corner of the square must just touch the edge of the cup. When the production period begins, fill the cups and cover them as quickly as possible. Cups must be completely full and covered to be sold, otherwise consumers will buy another brand of food cups and you'll be fired. You don't want to lose your job because of partially filled cups of food, or because profits at your factory are too low. What would your family say? They're counting on buying a new DVD player with your bonus!

Activity 1 (continued)

Manager 3

Congratulations! You have been promoted to the position of plant manager of the Good-4-You Food Company. All those years of hard work have paid off! Now you will earn a higher salary and share in the company's profits. Your factory fills and covers cups with foodstuffs. To produce one unit, pour the food mix to fill a cup completely to the top and then cover it. Do not touch the top or inside of the cups or the food mix that goes into the cups with your hands. Any food that drops outside of cups is contaminated and cannot be used. Fill as many cups as possible in the production period, which will last about one minute. The money the company gets from selling the cups pays for raw materials, labor, plant and equipment. Your company must also pay a tax on each unit of pollution it releases into the environment. The pollution will be measured. For each four inches of tape required to pick up your waste, you will be taxed one piece of candy. After all of those expenses are paid, what's left is profit. You will receive a base salary of three pieces of candy as long as you have this job. Your share of the profit will be one piece of candy for each cup filled after you have filled five cups. (For example, if you fill eight cups, you will receive three additional pieces of candies.) Your cups must be arranged in a straight line (like this: OOOOOO) before you begin to fill them. After you fill your cups, you must place a square paper cover over the food. Each corner of the square must just touch the edge of the cup. When the production period begins, fill the cups and cover them as quickly as possible. Cups must be completely full to be sold, otherwise consumers will buy another brand of food cups and you will be fired.

LESSON TWELVE
INCOME DISTRIBUTION AND REDISTRIBUTION POLICIES

INTRODUCTION

In a market system, the prices paid to owners of productive resources are determined by the interaction of supply and demand. Some productive resources have higher prices than others, and some households own more productive resources than others. Therefore, incomes will not be equally distributed across households in a market system.

One of the roles of government is to redistribute income to promote economic equity or fairness. If the distribution of income among households is considered inequitable, government policies may be used to redistribute income. These include changes in who pays taxes, and the level of benefits provided to some individuals and households through transfer payments (including welfare programs and social security) or programs that provide or partially subsidize education and training programs. However, because differences in income reflect differences in productivity and are powerful incentives for workers and firms, government policies to reduce inequality may weaken these incentives.

When countries experience drastic changes in their economic systems, they are likely to have major changes in the distribution of income as well as in levels of production (GDP), productivity, and prices. Since the breakup of the former Soviet Union, in the transition from command to market-based economies, many of the newly independent nations have seen rapid increases in income inequality.

CONCEPTS

Lorenz curve
Income distribution
Gini coefficient
Government redistribution policies

CONTENT STANDARDS

Income for most people is determined by the market value of the productive resources they sell. What workers earn depends, primarily, on the market value of what they produce and how productive they are.

BENCHMARKS

To earn income, people sell productive resources. These include their labor, capital, natural resources, and entrepreneurial talents.

A wage or salary is the price of labor; it usually is determined by the supply of and demand for labor.

Changes in the structure of the economy, the level of gross domestic product, technology, government policies, and discrimination can influence personal income.

OBJECTIVES

♦ Students construct a Lorenz curve to illustrate the distribution of income in an economy.

♦ Students explain the relationship between the Gini coefficient and the Lorenz curve.

♦ Students discuss the effects of government policies that redistribute income.

LESSON DESCRIPTION

Students learn how Lorenz curves and Gini coefficients are used to show the degree of income inequality in a national economy. These measures are then used to discuss such questions as:

How much income equality is desirable?

Do government policies that redistribute income affect incentives and economic efficiency?

How much income redistribution occurs when an economy changes from a command system to a market system?

TIME REQUIRED

One class period.

MATERIALS

- Activity 1: Lorenz Curves and the Distribution of Income, one copy for each student
- Activity 2: How Much Income (In)Equality Do We Want?, one copy for each student
- Activity 3: I Dream of Gini, one copy for each student

PROCEDURES

1. Distribute Activity 1 and have students read it. Complete the worksheet as a class exercise, explaining the calculations and the graph.

A. *(In the first table, the missing values for the cumulative shares of income are 14 and 55 percent. The graph is shown below.)*

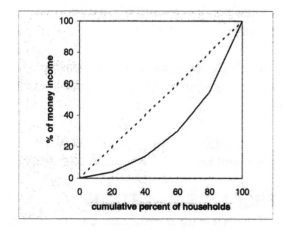

B. *(In the second table, the cumulative income percentages for perfect income equality are: 20; 40; 60; 80; 100. If you graphed correctly, the Lorenz curve*

is now a straight, diagonal line. One point on the Lorenz curve is (80, 80) where the poorest 80 percent of households earn 80 percent of the income. All other points on this Lorenz curve have "twin pair" coordinates, or

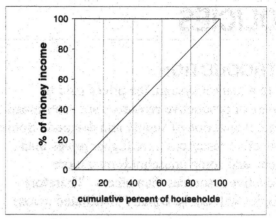

(X,Y) values which are numerically identical. As always, the Lorenz curve begins with the origin (0,0) and ends with (100,100).

Perfect equality of **income distribution** (the division of total income among households) does not exist in actual economies, nor is it necessarily a desirable redistribution goal. However, the diagonal line of equality does serve as a benchmark or standard of comparison. Inequality is measured by how far from the line of equality the actual Lorenz curve bows downward. The further below the diagonal the Lorenz curve is, the greater is the inequality of income distribution. If the Lorenz curve lies exactly on top of the diagonal line, there is perfect equality. If it lies so low that it follows the X-axis all the way horizontally to 100 and then one person or family gets all of the income in the nation, there is perfect inequality. Actual income distributions for countries fall somewhere in between perfect equality and perfect inequality.)

C. *(In the last graph for Activity 1, curve A shows more equality; curve B shows more inequality.)*

2. Distribute Activity 2. Have students complete their ideal distributions and think about the discussion questions for a few minutes. Then lead a class discussion on the four questions, touching on the following points:

A. It is unlikely that everyone will agree on the ideal distribution of income. Some will favor stronger financial incentives because they feel they are important for both the current and future performance of the economy, or because it is fair to let people keep most of what they earn. Others favor more government redistribution programs to assist low-income families based on humanitarian concerns, and sometimes because they feel that financial motivations are not as important in explaining who will work diligently. Adults, politicians, and for that matter economists often disagree on these questions.

B. Some form of redistribution programs has existed in every market economy, but the more extensive the redistribution programs become, the weaker property rights are in terms of people's claims to what they earn. The less people's incomes are tied to the market value of the productive resources they own (including their own labor), the less the economic system can be considered a pure market economy. It probably makes more sense to view this relationship on a continuum, rather than setting some hard and fast boundary that divides market and command economies. However, unless the ownership of productive resources is shared equally, and all of those resources have the same market value, a market economy will never exhibit a perfectly equal distribution of income.

C. The pursuit of income equality in the former Soviet Union – even though it

was never fully achieved – is often noted as one reason for the poor incentives and generally poor level of economic efficiency achieved in that system, although there are certainly many other important reasons for those failings. (See the introductory essay for this volume by George Horwich.)

D. The final discussion question is, in many ways, the real heart of the debate among economists, politicians, and the public at large about the appropriate level or extent for government programs that redistribute income from high-income to low-income families. Another part of that debate, that goes beyond the purview of this volume, is how to design redistribution programs that maintain incentives for people to work, save, and invest – both for those who pay the taxes to fund these programs, as well as for those who receive payments or other benefits from the programs.

As background information for this discussion, or as a way to wrap up the discussion, you may want to inform the class that in 1998, the cumulative distribution of shares of money income in the United States (as reported by the Bureau of Census), not considering taxes paid or the value of government benefits received (which would make the distribution somewhat more equal), was: Quintile 1, 3.6 percent; Quintiles 1 and 2, 12.6 percent; Quintiles 1-3, 27.6 percent; Quintiles 1-4, 50.8 percent; and Quintiles 1-5, 100 percent).

3. Distribute Activity 3.

A. *(For the perfect equality scenario, area A would be zero, and the Gini coefficient would be: 0/(0+B) = 0. In general, when the distribution of income is highly uniform or equal, the Gini coefficient is small and approaches zero.)*

B. *(For the Gill Bates scenario, the Lorenz curve would be very flat and low, hugging the X-axis until the very end, when it would zoom up to the (100,100) point (Gill being in the fifth quintile, of course). Area B, below the Lorenz curve, is just a speck in the lower right corner of the graph. Consider it small enough to be valued as zero.*

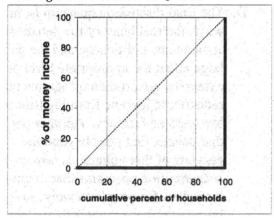

Area A is almost the entire space under the diagonal line. In other words, as B approaches 0, the Gini coefficient approaches the numerical value of 1, or Gini = A/(A+0) = 1. Therefore, the Gini ratio has a range from 0, for perfect equality, to 1, for perfect inequality. Larger Gini values indicate greater income inequality.

C. *(The Gini coefficients from the transition economies showed rising income inequality over that period.)*

D. *(In time, the hope is that market reforms will lead to higher income levels for families in all income quintiles.)*

CLOSURE

Ask the following questions:

1. Do you believe young people or old people in the United States are more likely to favor more equality in the distribution of income, and more government redistribution programs to promote equality? Why?

2. Do you believe young people or old people in the former Soviet Union are more likely to favor more equality in the distribution of income, and more government redistribution programs to promote equality? Why?

In the United States, younger people often favor more equality and government programs to redistribute income. That may mean that people become somewhat more conservative, politically, as they grow older. It almost certainly reflects the fact that households headed by middle-aged and older adults tend to have higher incomes (at least until retirement) than households headed by younger adults.

In the former Soviet Union, market reforms were accompanied by hyperinflation that sharply reduced the value of pensions paid by the state to retirees. Therefore, in these countries, the elderly have become one of the largest groups seeking new programs to redistribute income, or the reinstatement of old programs at levels closer to their former value.

ASSESSMENT

Have students draw Lorenz curves for the 1998 cumulative distribution of income data provided at the end of procedure 2. On the same graph, draw the Lorenz curve for their ideal distribution of income, from Activity 2. Have students write two or three paragraphs based on these Lorenz curves, explaining whether their ideal distribution calls for greater equality or inequality of income than the actual distribution of income, and what kinds changes in government tax or spending programs they would support to redistribute income to achieve their ideal distribution.

Activity 1
Lorenz Curves and the Distribution of Income

The **Lorenz curve**, named for the statistician M. O. Lorenz, is a graphical representation of the distribution of national income. The horizontal axis measures the cumulative percentage of families in the nation, ranked from poorest to richest. The vertical axis measures the cumulative percentage of money income. The number of families is usually measured in quintiles, or fifths, so there are five groups of households shown on the horizontal axis: the poorest 20 percent of families (first quintile), the poorest 40 percent (first and second quintiles), the poorest 60 percent (first, second, and third quintiles), the poorest 80 percent (first through fourth quintiles), and finally 100 percent (all five quintiles). The Lorenz curve is plotted by showing the cumulative income share for each of the quintiles. For example, when graphing the point for the poorest 60 percent of households, the vertical height is determined by adding the income shares of the first three quintiles. The first point of the Lorenz curve is always the origin (0,0) because zero percent of families receive zero percent of total family income. The last point of the Lorenz curve is always (100, 100) because 100 percent of families receive 100 percent of cumulative family income.

A. Convert the income distribution data below to cumulative shares to find the missing entries in the table. Then plot the cumulative share points (the last column), using the graph provided. Connect the points to form the Lorenz curve. Hint: the points all lie below the dotted diagonal line and form a curve that appears to bow downward.

Hypothetical Income Distribution

Quintile	Percent Share of Money Income	Cumulative Percent of Families	Cumulative Percentage Share of Money Income
0	0.0	0	0.0
1	4.0	20	4.0
2	10.0	40	___
3	16.0	60	30.0
4	25.0	80	___
5	45.0	100	100.0

Lorenz Curve for Hypothetical Income Distribution

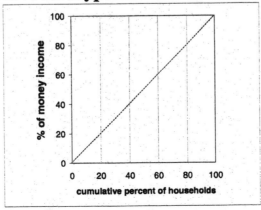

Activity 1 (continued)

   B. What would the Lorenz curve look like if all households had the same money income? Each quintile would have the same share of income, as shown in the second column of the table below. Calculate values for the last column to determine cumulative shares of income under this assumption of perfect income equality.

Q	% Share Income	Cumulative % Families	Cumulative % Income
1	20.0	20	___
2	20.0	40	___
3	20.0	60	___
4	20.0	80	___
5	20.0	100	___

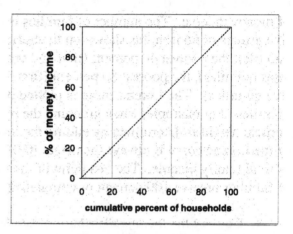

Using the figures from the last column, graph this special case of the Lorenz curve in the space provided to the right.

   C. Based on the two Lorenz curves you have drawn, would you say that curve A or curve B in the graph below represents an economy with greater income equality? Why?

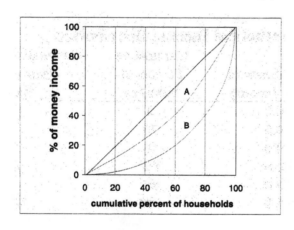

Activity 2
How Much Income (In)Equality Do We Want?

Wages and profits are powerful incentives in market economies. The chance to earn more money motivates many people to work hard, master difficult skills that require years of study or experience, and accept the risks involved in producing goods and services that consumers may or may not want to purchase at prices high enough to cover the costs of production. These incentives play an important role in making the economy work well. If there is competition among many workers and firms for high wages and profits, goods and services will be produced efficiently, that is producing things that consumers really want to buy, producing them at the lowest possible cost, and selling them at the lowest possible prices.

But what about the people who cannot or will not compete for high wages or profits, including people who are very young or very old, and people with severe mental or physical disabilities? How can they buy food, clothing, shelter, medical care, education, and other goods and services? In all modern economies, whether they are market or command economies, there are national **government redistribution policies** for shifting income to low-income families. This is usually done in two ways: 1) by providing money and/or some kinds of goods and services to low-income families, and 2) by taxing low-income families at relatively lower levels or rates (or perhaps not taxing them at all), while taxing high-income families at higher levels or rates.

When the government redistributes income using these policies, one result is that it reduces the financial incentives to work, save, and invest. That represents what economists often describe as a tradeoff between efficiency and income equality. Your class will discuss several questions about this tradeoff, but first indicate in the table below what share of national income you believe each quintile (20 percent of families) would receive if there was an ideal distribution of income in your national economy. Quintile 1 is the 20 percent of families with the lowest incomes; Quintile 5 is the 20 percent of families with the highest incomes. Consider the tradeoff between equality and efficiency as you fill in this table. Remember, the larger the share of income received by upper-income families (Quintiles 4 and 5), the stronger the financial incentives to work, save, and invest. That will lead to greater efficiency in production, lower prices for goods and services, and more economic growth in the future. But at the same time, if upper-income families receive a larger share of national income, lower-income families (Quintiles 1 and 2) will receive smaller shares.

Quintile	Ideal Share of National Income Received (%)
1 (20% of families with lowest incomes)	_____
2	_____
3	_____
4	_____
5 (20% of families with highest incomes)	_____

Activity 2 (continued)

Discussion Questions:

A.   Do you believe everyone in the class will agree about the most desirable distribution of income? If not, will most of the disagreement be about how much income the upper, lower, or middle quintiles should receive? Do you often hear adults, or political candidates and leaders, disagreeing about these kinds of issues? Explain your answers to these questions.

B.   Can you really have a market economy in which the distribution of income is perfectly equal? Why or why not?

C.   Do you believe the fall of the command economies in the former Soviet Union was in any way related to attempts to maintain income equality? Explain your answer.

D.   What helps low-income families more: to redistribute income through government tax and spending programs, or to encourage economic growth so that more goods and services will be produced for all families to consume in the future? Explain your answer.

Activity 3
I Dream of Gini

The **Gini coefficient** is a ratio measuring the equality of income distribution calculated by using the areas around the Lorenz curve. In the graph at the right, area A is the area below the straight diagonal line that indicates perfect income equality, but above the Lorenz curve. Area B is the area below the Lorenz curve. The formula for the Gini coefficient is: $G = (A/(A+B))$.

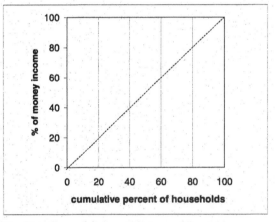

   A. If the actual distribution of income is perfectly equal, the Lorenz curve will lie directly on top of the straight diagonal line. In this case, what is the numerical value for A, and for the Gini coefficient?

   B. Suppose a wealthy person named Gill Bates earns nearly all the income in the United States. Draw the Lorenz curve for that situation on the bottom graph, and then estimate the value for that Gini coefficient.

   C. During the first years of the transition from command to market economies, the countries in eastern Europe and the former Soviet Union saw their Gini coefficients rise by several points. For example, in Bulgaria the Gini coefficient rose from .23 to .34; in the Czech Republic, from .19 to .27; in Hungary, from .21 to .23; in Poland, from .25 to .30; and in Slovenia from .24 to .28. Do these higher Gini coefficents represent a movement toward more equality or more inequality of income in these countries?

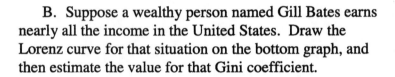

   D. During the transition from command to market economies, which people or families would be likely to gain income, and which would be likely to lose income? In 20-30 years, will income levels be higher or lower in these countries than they would have been if the transition to market-based economies had not been made? Which families will probably have more or less income at that time, compared to income levels before the transition?